Countryside Herbs

Countryside Herbs

Rosamond Richardson

PIATKUS

© 1985 Rosamond Richardson

First published in 1985 by
Judy Piatkus (Publishers) Limited, London

British Library Cataloguing in Publication Data

Richardson, Rosamond
  Countryside herbs.
  1. Herbs
  I. Title
  641.3'57   SB351.H5

  ISBN 0-86188-367-5

Edited by Susan Fleming
Designed and illustrated by Zena Flax

Typeset by Tradespools Ltd, Frome, Somerset
Printed and bound by The Bath Press, Avon

Contents

For William

in memory of a certain herb garden

About herbs

This book is about the stories and legends that have been woven around
herbs over the centuries by country folk. Although the original sources of
the myths and folklore are obscure, most of them are European – a fact
hardly surprising when one realizes that many of the plants are native to
the Mediterranean and the near East. Some have far more folklore than
others, and the famous British quartet – parsley, sage, rosemary and thyme
– have the most. Yet they all have their own individual quality and
fascination, and in an age when oral country traditions are fast dying out, it
seems right to rescue them from oblivion, for they reveal fascinating
insights into the way our forebears lived. As soon as early man discovered
that these plants were useful to him as well as being pleasing to his senses,
herbs and wild plants began to play an important role in everyday life,
from cooking, medicine, aromatics and beauty care, to other, less ordinary,
aspects of life such as the realms of superstition, magic, enchantment and
religious ritual.

The myths and magic of herbs

Perhaps the potency of herbs in magic derived from their highly effective
medicinal uses. Consequently, in early societies these natural healers came
to merit the honour of being dedicated to the gods, and gradually legends
came to be woven around particular deities and their corresponding
plants. An ambivalence arises which appears time and time again: on the
one hand a herb is holy and propitious; on the other, a demonic
ingredient of a magic spell. Certain herbs were involved in specific
ceremonies both sacred and profane; they were used to sanctify a temple –
or to invoke the Evil Eye.

    The Druids picked herbs with great reverence. Dressed in white linen robes, with no shoes on, they cut especially precious herbs with a gold blade. It was considered most effective of all to pick herbs naked, at or just after the full moon.

The country wife came to have a great respect for herbs, for they were her medicine chest. She, too, was careful how she picked them. She would always use her left hand, never use an iron tool, never face into the wind or look behind her whilst gathering. If she dropped herbs on to the ground, she believed that their strength leaked back into the earth, and to get the best out of them she would talk to them – tell them, in effect, what she was doing. To the country wife, the term 'herb' meant a green plant without a woody stem, so her lore applied to wild flowers and 'weeds' as well as to the culinary herbs.

Ancient tradition said that all herbs should be sown or planted during the first or second quarter of the moon, and it was a small step from these superstitions to the place herbs attained in the Middle Ages in the magic artillery of witches' spells and potions. Herb garlands were hung on the door of the house on certain saints' days: particular plants were believed to possess special powers to avert evil spirits, to protect the house from lightning or keep witches away. Many a cowherd would hang a bunch of herbs by the dairy door to stop the milk from turning sour, or prevent it from being bewitched.

Exactly how and where all this mythology started is obscure, but presumably it arose from the close connection in early society between magic and medicine. A plant that could cure an illness must have special powers bestowed on it by gods or devils, and from the earliest times it is clear that man recognized the medicinal properties of herbs. Ancient tablets found in the library of Assurbanipal, King of Assyria from 668–626 BC show that his medical men were familiar with the properties of up to 250 plant drugs, which included many still used today: poppy, belladonna, henbane, mandrake, garlic, onions, hemp and saffron.

The ancient Egyptians used herbs to embalm the Pharaohs, and left them in their tombs to ensure a safe journey to the hereafter. Greeks and Romans held herbs in sacred esteem and used them in their forms of worship: they decorated altars with them, wore them at weddings to bestow good luck, or strewed them at funerals to symbolize eternal life, and used them as incense. Both the Greeks and the Romans wore garlands of herbs at feasts and banquets, believing that by so doing they would avoid a hangover! The Greeks crowned the winners of their various games with bay, fennel and parsley, and the Romans bestowed honours on both worthy citizens and victorious warriors by presenting them with herbal wreaths and crowns.

The Greeks evolved a system of plant symbolism which became a fine art. They could conduct secret conversations by exchanging garlands, bouquets or posies, as every herb had a specific meaning such as fidelity, doubt, pleasure or jealousy. This tradition was passed on down through the centuries in western Europe and became popular in the courts of medieval France. It became the language of lovers and was used by poets and mystics. Much of it is forgotten today, but the late Victorian era revelled in it and recorded it in books on the 'Language of Flowers'.

The early Greeks also knew of the healing powers of plants. The philosopher Aristotle (384–322 BC) and his pupil and friend Theophrastus (c.370–286 BC) attempted to work out a scientific system of plants, and the latter's *Enquiry into Plants* had a profound effect on the emerging study of botany. However, it was the earliest researcher, Hippocrates (c.460–377 BC), who was to earn the title of 'Father of Modern Medicine': he was the first man to separate demonology from medical practice, and among his 400 simples, or herbal preparations, are many remedies that we still use today.

The significance of the dual nature of herbal plants – in magic and medicine – culminated in a remarkable book, *De Materia Medica* (c. AD 77) by Dioscorides (see page 14). *De Materia Medica* was to influence the thinking of healers and their use of plant drugs for 1,500 years. The work names 600 plants, many of which are still featured in modern pharmacopoeias. He says, for example, that dried coltsfoot leaves, smoked through a reed, will clear mucus and catarrh, and this remedy was still being used by country folk until recently. Some of his cures are less convincing, notably those to counter the 'bitings of madde dogges' or the stings of venomous serpents! Some of his remedies for rheumatism are no less far-fetched, but for all that they make good reading.

When the Romans invaded Britain in the first century AD they brought with them many of the herbs we know today. But the scholarly achievements of the classical world were soon forgotten after the fall of Rome. During the Dark Ages in Europe, knowledge of herbs was kept alive largely in the monasteries, where many monks were practising physicians and had their own infirmaries. Some tended the physic garden, whilst others copied out manuscripts from the ancient writers. Outside the monasteries, magic and superstition held sway, with travelling herb women and healers doing much to discredit their trade. A few herbals

hyssop

spearmint

were written in manuscript during this time, and the first one in the vernacular was called *The Leech Boke of Bald.* The most significant work of all was Saint Albertus Magnus' *Boke of Secretes* (see page 15).

The great age of the herbal dawned with a new age revolutionized by the invention of printing. In England this revival was marked by the love that the Tudors had for their herbs. They were great gardeners and this was the heyday of the knot-garden and of dwarf mazes hedged with evergreen herbs like rosemary, thyme, lavender and winter savory. In them they grew a wide variety of simples – marjoram, hyssop, fennel, santolina and rue. They made teas, cordials and syrups with hyssop and fennel, and concocted inspired salads or 'sallets' using herbs, fresh flowers and buds, nuts and mushrooms and wild salading leaves. They made medicines and tonics from herbs, and the bees that loved these herbs provided the housewife with her honey.

One of King Henry VIII's favourite hobbies was the concocting of herbal remedies, and his Court Apothecary was a man of standing in the society of the day, traditionally garbed in a green robe to mark his learning in the virtues of plants. Until the time of James I, apothecaries belonged to the same city guild as the pepperers or grocers, and they congregated mainly in Bucklersbury, the one part of London to escape the plague – probably because it was so heavily perfumed with herbs, gums and spices, all of which have antiseptic properties.

The great herbals of the sixteenth and seventeenth centuries followed the pattern set by Dioscorides, much of whose material they plagiarized. In a sense this was invaluable since it meant that this ancient legacy was no longer under threat of extinction. These herbals, therefore, set down in print for the first time much age-old folklore, myths and legends. They increased a general awareness of the usefulness of herbs at the same time as rekindling an ancient oral tradition. The greatest trio of these writers were William Turner, John Gerard and John Parkinson (see pages 16 and 17).

The seventeenth century saw a different approach to herbalism, epitomized by the herbal of Nicholas Culpeper (1616–54). He incorporated into his writings the thinking of Paracelsus (see page 12) who had re-introduced an astrological element into herbal practice, a facet neglected since the time of ancient Babylon.

The work of the Swedish botanist, Linnaeus (1707–78), in classifying plants is of considerable help in tracing the old myths and powers of herbs, since the botanical Latin names he gave them reflect their

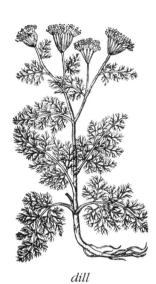

dill

various legends or attributes. For example, tansy is *tanecetum* from the Greek *athanatos*, immortal, because this herb was thought to confer immortality on anyone who ate it, and it was also an embalming herb with antiseptic and therefore preservative properties. Sage is *salvia officinalis*: *salvere* means to be in good health and *officinalis* denotes the approval of its use in medicine by medical practitioners.

The common names of herbs given to them by country folk also give us clues as to their folklore and mythology. Lovage is also called 'Love Parsley' from a belief that it had an aphrodisiac effect if eaten. Tarragon is 'herb of the dragon', *estragon* in French, and gets its specific name *dranunculus* from the Latin *draco* 'little dragon', because it was thought to cure the bites and sting of venomous animals. These descriptive local names given to herbs and wild plants give charming and endearing clues to the stories behind them.

Herbs in folk medicine

As far as man's experience is concerned, it is open to conjecture whether the medicinal properties of herbs were discovered as a result of their culinary uses, or vice versa. Certainly early man must have observed how animals reacted to eating plants, either by being sick, dying, recovering from sickness or wounds, or simply remaining healthy. No doubt the herb's aroma had much to do with the way man was attracted to them in the first place: a pungent aroma indicates the presence of essential oil, a powerful substance which can be used most obviously in perfumery and in aromatherapy, but also in flavouring foods or, originally by trial and error, in medical practice. Medical herbalism is an ancient science made reputable by its antiquity, although it has seen periods in its history when quacks and rogues have discredited it.

Earlier this century plant drugs were overshadowed by the advent of synthetic drugs, but the latter's frequently unpleasant and unpredictable side-effects have led scientists back to analyse plants using modern analysis techniques. Their findings are interesting, sometimes surprising, in the light of the old wives' tales which they appear to verify. There is currently a revival in medical herbalism, backed by this up-to-date scientific research which is investigating anew the properties of plants which have been used by man for thousands of years.

One of the most interesting historical aberrations in the areas of quackery which loom from time to time in the history of herbal medicine, was the 'Doctrine of Signatures'. This was a kind of sympathetic magic which, although older, is closely connected with the name Paracelsus (1493–1541). He certainly did not invent it, but went all the way to persuade his contemporaries of its absolute truth. His knowledge of botany was meagre, but he proclaimed that all herbs were put on earth by God for man's use. They were each stamped with a clear sign or signature by Him, thus making it clear for what purpose they were designed. A plant with a heart-shaped leaf would cure cardiac complaints; a yellow flower indicated a remedy for bilious disorders; and you could use a plant with kidney-shaped parts for the renal system. The walnut, with its crinkly brown surface, must be good for a brain injury, and the willow, because it grows in damp places, would surely cure rheumatism.

Paracelsus was also a firm believer in astrology and the influence of the planets and stars over plants. Every plant was under the influence of one particular star which would draw it out of the earth and cause it to germinate. Not only was the herb influenced, but so were different parts of the body relating to the herb. Like the Doctrine of Signatures, this idea was not original, for the ancient Babylonians had formulated and believed in a system of astrological botany.

Paracelsus, or Theophrastus Bombastus von Hohenheim, was a doctor, and for a short while professor at Basle. He lost both his job and the respect of his colleagues when he ordered the works of Galen and others to be burned, declaring, 'I shall be the monarch, and mine shall the monarchy be.' But the study of botany was infected with his thinking, and only as magic came to be divorced from medicine once more in the eighteenth century did Paracelsus become discredited.

The range of medicinal properties ascribed to herbs is very wide, so it is impossible to generalize about their healing qualities. What is certain, however, is that there is an increasing interest in herbalism as witnessed by the growth of alternative or complementary movements in medicine. The science of aromatherapy is also seeing a revival – the skills of using the essential oils of plants in healing, for improving the appearance of skin and hair, and for enhancing sensuality. An offshoot of this is the use of oils to create atmosphere or mood – specific herbs being used to promote well-being and contentment, or activity and inspiration, for example.

Attributes that medical herbs have in common are that they are both tonic and stimulant, notably coriander and fennel. A large number are sedative, having a tranquillizing and soothing effect. Balm, borage, basil, chamomile, lavender, sage, and thyme were all widely used for depression, to cheer the despondent and banish melancholia.

Another area in which herbs have healing powers is in chest complaints. Basil, bay, lavender, marjoram and thyme are all expectorants and so are used to loosen a cough, whereas bergamot, sage and tansy are good in a gargle for sore throats. Bergamot and thyme contain a volatile oil 'thymol' which acts effectively on pleurisy, tuberculosis, bronchitis, asthma and catarrh.

Many herbs act on the stomach as a digestive, especially parsley, chives, lovage, rosemary, fennel, thyme and marjoram. These last three are also carminative, or relieve flatulence, as do bergamot, lovage, coriander and mint. Mint, fennel and dill are good for gripes: lavender, marigold, bergamot and mint help symptoms of nausea. Bay is a powerful laxative, and quite a few of the herbs are diuretic – fennel, lovage, parsley, thyme, rue and rosemary being the most powerful to act on the kidneys.

For rheumatism and gout, lovage, tansy, rue, marjoram and rosemary found their way into folk medicine, and borage was prescribed for a weak heart. For minor complaints like bites and stings, borage, marigold, hyssop, sage and rue were recommended: their leaves were rubbed into the affected parts. Marjoram was for earache, and lavender, mint and thyme for a headache. Marigold, rue and thyme were all considered good for skin disorders; borage, hyssop and rue as eye lotions. Borage and sage were 'good for the heart', tansy got rid of worms and, made up into a poultice, borage, chamomile and sage would bring down inflammations.

Herbs were widely used as antiseptics, their strong essential oil believed to combat bacteria. The major cleansing herbs were lovage, marjoram, sage, rosemary, mint, lavender and thyme. These two latter herbs, along with rue and hyssop, were also applied to burns, cuts, bruises and open wounds to help them heal.

Infusions, decoctions and poultices
The principal methods of application for medicinal herbs were (and are), an infusion or decoction for internal use, and a compress or poultice for external use.

An infusion is made by placing $\frac{1}{2}$ oz/15 g of the required dried herb in a warm cup, and pouring over 1 pint/600 ml boiling water. If using fresh herbs, the ratio is 1 oz/30 g to 1 pint/600 ml boiling water. Cover tightly and stand for 5–10 minutes before straining. Sweeten with honey if desired. A decoction is made by soaking the dried herb in cold water for 10 minutes, using the same ratio as for an infusion, using an enamel and not a metal saucepan. Bring to the boil, covered, and simmer for 2–3 minutes, then allow to steep for 10 minutes, still covered. Cool and strain.

For external use, a poultice is made by bruising the fresh plant and pulping it, then it is mixed with hot water and applied to the affected area. If using dried herbs, they should be mixed with a paste made of flour or bran and water, to the ratio of 2 oz/60 g dried herb to 1 pint/600 ml paste. Bandage this paste to the injury. Alternatively a compress can be made by bringing 1–2 heaped tablespoons of the herb to the boil in 1 cup of water, covered. Steep for 5 minutes, still covered, then dip cotton wool or gauze into it and apply it to the damaged part and cover it with a bandage. When the compress has lost its heat, repeat the process.

The great herbalists

Pliny and Galen

Pliny the Elder lived from AD 23–79 and was the most influential writer on plants in ancient Rome. His *Natural History* runs to 37 volumes and is a compilation of 2,000 Greek and Roman treatises. Much of the work is dedicated to the medical uses of plants, although there is also a great deal of folklore in it, and it became one of the chief scientific authorities of the European Middle Ages.

Galen (AD 129–c.199) became second only to his great master and countryman, Hippocrates, as a practising physician, philosopher and philologist. He wrote numerous books, including a herbal, and his ideas embraced two major concepts: the idea of the unity of the organism, and that a good doctor should also be a philosopher. He agreed with Aristotle that 'Nature does nothing in vain', and his teachings had a profound effect on the development of western science during the Renaissance.

Pedanius Dioscorides (1st century AD)

Dioscorides was a Greek physician to the Roman army and the first real medical botanist. There is conjecture that he was also personal physician to Anthony and Cleopatra. His book, *De Materia Medica*, was based on personal findings gathered in his travels, rather than on hearsay, and so his observations were all first-hand. He incorporated into his book all the available earlier writings on plants such as those of Theophrastus and Hippocrates.

The Dark Ages

The *Herbarium* of Apuleius Platonicus (about whom nothing is known) was written in the fifth century AD, but was not published until the fifteenth century, from an old manuscript. It became the first work through which any systematic knowledge of plants was brought to Britain. The first herbal in the vernacular, *The Leech Boke of Bald*, was written between 900 and 950. Bald was reputed to be a friend of King Alfred, and his book is based not on classical texts but rather on local knowledge and herb lore. A monk, John of Gaddesdon, wrote the first major book on botanical medicine to come out of the early Middle Ages: *Rosa Anglica* (1314–17) combined Greek, Arabic and Saxon sources as well as observations based on personal clinical experience.

Albertus Magnus (1193–1280)

Albert, Count of Bollstadt and Bishop of Ratisbon, was a remarkable German who became a saint. He was a scholar of zoology, mineralogy and botany, and also had a reputation as a philosopher; he was a traveller and writer, a lecturer in theology at Rome, a friend and teacher of St Thomas Aquinas, and a plant-collector. His seven volumes on botany describe for the first time the flora of Europe which he recorded on his travels: the veins and geometric designs of leaves, the habitats and growth of plants. He came within a whisker of suggesting a system of classification for plants, and his minute observation of the details of plants reveals an unprecedented talent for morphology. But the potential of his ideas in his *Boke of Secretes* was not recognized nor realized until Linnaeus, some 400 years later.

The first modern herbals

The invention of the printing press in the late fifteenth century revolutionized intellectual scholarship. Early *Herbarii* in Latin and German, and the *Hortus Sanitatis* of 1491 are forerunners of the later great herbals, and herald an age when people began to examine and study the plants they were writing about instead of copying ancient manuscripts. In 1526 *The Grete Herball* was translated from the French *Le Grand Herbier*, exposing quacks for selling fake drugs and warning the public to 'eschew ye frawde of them that selleth it'.

Banckes' Herball of 1525 has a personal and individual charm even though it is unillustrated. In 1527 *The Vertuous Boke of Distillacyoun of the waters of all manners of Herbes* was printed 'in the Flete Strete by me Laurens Andrewe, in the signe of the golden Crosse'. All these minor herbals were precursors of the great works of Dodoens in the Netherlands, and William Turner, John Gerard and John Parkinson in England.

Rembert Dodoens (1517–85)

Dodoens was born in the Low Countries and studied astronomy, botany and geography at Louvain. He qualified as a doctor and was appointed personal physician to Emperor Maximilian II. He ended his career as the professor of medicine at Leyden. His *Cruydeboeck* of 1554 classifies plants according to their properties and affinities, rather than alphabetically, and indicates the habitats and localities of plants and their times of flowering. It was translated into French, and then, by Henry Lyte (born c.1529), into English. This appeared in 1578 under the title *A Niewe Herbal or Historie of Plantes*. Dodoens' other botanical work, *Pemptades* (1583), was translated into English by Priest, with a complete glossary of botanical terms, and this text was the one that John Gerard purloined and reproduced as his own work.

William Turner (c.1510–68)

Known as the 'Father of English Botany' Turner was born in Morpeth, Northumberland, the son of a tanner. He studied medicine at Pembroke College, Cambridge, and became a Protestant clergyman, for which he was persecuted, spending several years in exile. He travelled widely, studying plants scientifically. He was acutely aware of the general ignorance surrounding plant names, both in the vernacular and in Latin and Greek. In 1548 he produced *The Names of Herbes*, and his *New Herball* of 1551 was dedicated to Queen Elizabeth I. He arranged his plants alphabetically and his text shows his independent thinking and his intolerance (on the whole) of superstition.

John Gerard (1545–1612)

Born in Nantwich in Cheshire, Gerard became a 'Master of Chirurgerie, or barber-surgeon. He was also a very successful gardener, exercising his skills on his garden in Holborn (then a fashionable quarter of London), and tending Lord Burghley's gardens in The Strand for twenty years.

In 1597 his *Herball* was published, the outcome of a disreputable sequence of events. Gerard had plagiarized Priest's translation of Dodoens' *Pemptades*, although he claims in his preface that the work had disappeared when its author died. He published it as his own work, merely altering the arrangement from that of Dodoens to that of the herbal of Matthias de l'Obel (1538–1616), published in 1570. De l'Obel (after whom the lobelia is named) was physician to William of Orange and botanist to James I. What is more, Gerard's knowledge of botany was so meagre that he could not couple the woodblocks with their appropriate descriptions, and so de l'Obel was called in by the printer to correct his blunders. Up until that time the two men had been friends, but after a while Gerard grew impatient and stopped the work on the grounds that de l'Obel had forgotten his English!

Gerard was rather a rogue, but by all accounts a likeable one with a wide circle of friends. The importance of his *Herball* is chiefly in an improved edition brought out in 1633 by Thomas Johnson. He corrected many of the errors, enlarged it to include 2,850 plants, and illustrated it with new woodcuts.

marigold

John Parkinson (1567–1650)

John Parkinson was the last great British herbalist of the period, and he had a famous garden in London. He was apothecary to James I and botanist to Charles I. In 1629 his *Paradisi in Sole Paradisus Terrestris* was published, its title being a pun on the name of the author: 'Park in Sun'. It is actually more of a gardening book than a herbal and the illustrations are partly original and partly taken from de l'Obel. In 1640 he produced *Theatrum Botanicum* or 'Theatre of Plants', which is in effect a garden of simples. Although there is no attempt still at the classification of plants, the account of each one's nomenclature is detailed and full.

Nicholas Culpeper (1616–54)

Nicholas Culpeper set up as an astrologer and physician in Spitalfields around 1640. He was thoroughly disliked by the medical profession, whom he called 'a company of proud, insulting, domineering Doctors, whose wits were born about five hundred years before themselves'. One can detect the influence of Paracelsus (see page 12) in more ways than one. Culpeper went on to write a famous best-seller based on the propositions put forward by Paracelsus. It describes astrological influences on plants and, by the Doctrine of Signatures, the related parts of the body. It corresponds with the signs of the zodiac too: if a plant is ruled by Mars, the ruler of Aries, the plant would also come under the sign of Aries. Aries governs the head, and so it would follow that herbs governed by Aries would relieve ills of the head.

This herbal enjoyed enormous popularity and credence in its time and has been reprinted many times down the centuries. It seems preposterous that the name of an intellectual charlatan should be synonymous with herbs in the public mind, when other work being done both then and since can claim both the quality and scholarship which Culpeper's herbal lacks. However, never at a loss for words in his own defence, he insists in his introduction that he surpasses all his predecessors in that he is guided by reason alone, and all previous writers are 'as full of nonsense as an Egg is full of meat'.

Linnaeus (1707–78)

As Edward Lear puts it:

'There once was a chap called Linnaeus
Who discovered all nature was chaos.
He set out to describe
Every species and tribe
So that chaos would no longer dismay us.'

Carl von Linné was born in Sweden, the son of a pastor who had destined him for the church. But as a young man he was determined to study medicine, and was eventually appointed to the chair of medicine and botany at Uppsala where he remained for thirty-six years. In his early twenties he travelled through Lapland to record its flora, and returned resolved to sort out the chaos that reigned in the naming of plants, animals and minerals.

Linnaeus grouped plants into twenty-four classes according to the number of their stamens, and also their relative lengths and other characteristics. These were subdivided into 'orders' by the number of pistils. He gave two Latin names to each individual plant, one a general one identifying the group to which it belonged, the other a specific one to distinguish it from another within the same class. He published his work in a series of three volumes which culminated in *Species Plantarum* in 1753, and a saying was coined: 'Deus creavit, Linnaeus disposuit' (God created, Linnaeus put in order)!

The pleasures of a herb garden

bay tree

Perhaps it is in the area of gardening that the magic of herbs is as potent today as it ever was. On whatever scale, be it humble or majestic, a herb garden has its own beauty, its particular fascination. Its enchantment lies in the variety of foliage colour, its delightful flowers and above all its aromas, ranging from the sweetest imaginable to rancid and sour. Bees and butterflies are attracted to their nectar, and one of the old wives' favourites, the toad, appears still to like the shelter of certain herbs. (I have one as a regular visitor and whether or not he makes for the rue – see page 97 – is hard to say, but it is a delight to have him in my garden.)

Early herb gardens were entirely practical. Herbs were grown as 'useful plants', either for their medical or culinary properties. They were planted in rows much as we would plant vegetables today, and to this day a typical 'physic garden', such as the one at Chelsea in London, grows herbs in classified beds. The first herb gardens in England were grown for monastic infirmaries, and the plants used to tend the sick. Later on, with the growth of creative gardening, formal herb gardens came into their own, either in great settings like the parterres at Villandry, or simply a humble villager's plot. The Tudors delighted in the 'knot garden' where beds were laid out in geometric shapes and outlined with hedging of box, hyssop or lavender, making beds of varying shapes containing separately medicinal or culinary herbs.

In many ways herbs lend themselves to garden design because they are hardy, quick growers, and many of them are evergreen. They grow so rampantly that the garden looks luxuriant and colourful most of the year round. A herb garden is a source of pleasure to create as well as to enjoy, and can be a very simple thing to make. Once you have chosen your site, decide whether you will make a formal pattern for it, or whether you wish to design it in an informal manner. The first herb garden I ever made began with a small rectangular shape. I simply put a statue in the centre and laid four paved paths leading up to it. Within a year it was established as if it had been there for ever, not to mention how enchantingly pretty it looked.

Herbs will grow on most soils and do fairly well in our English climate so long as they get what sun is available, but they don't like being spoiled: you can kill them with kindness so it is best not to feed the soil too much or to over-water. Dead-head them after flowering, and cut back the deciduous herbs at the onset of winter, trimming the evergreens to a neat size. Try to plan your planting with the final height of the herb in mind, and design it around the relative greens of the different foliages, grouping or separating flower colour as desired.

In my original garden I planted lemon balm next to scarlet bergamot, with golden marjoram around it. In the next bed hyssop and lavender and borage gave striking contrasts of blues, mauves and grey-greens, underplanted with mint-green pennyroyal. I put rue and tansy together, one blue-green in leaf, the other the freshest of greens, and surrounded it with purple-flowering thyme. In the fourth bed were handsome chives, dark-green winter savory and pink-flowering marjoram always buzzing with bees. If you want to attract more bees to the garden, plant balm, the bee-plant, which acts like a magnet to them. Bees also love thyme, coriander and hyssop. To bring butterflies to your herb garden, plant lavender, catmint and Chinese chives, and they will make for the hyssop and the marjoram along with the bees.

Mints I have always planted well away from the herb garden, not wanting to invite a take-over bid. It is best to try to enclose them as much as possible, for example along a wall or path – or enclose them in a plastic container with drainage holes. In the wild garden with a pond or stream, put them down by the water's edge. Parsley, chervil and coriander I have always grown amongst the vegetables for, with all due respect, they are not the loveliest of herbs, yet I would not be without them in the kitchen. Basil I grow in pots indoors or in the greenhouse, and bay trees do well in tubs, accentuating the formal effect of a herb garden.

Another successful way to grow herbs is to dot them amongst border plants in the garden, again being aware of their final height and foliage colour. A cottage garden lends itself to this approach: along the edge of a border of typical cottage garden flowers plant thyme or hyssop, and give the pathways lavender hedges. If there is a rockery, then creeping thyme or pennyroyal makes ideal spreading cover. Amongst the

borage

herbaceous plants put rosemary, lovage, tansy, rue and all the different sages, and let marigolds and borage run everywhere. A patch of dill is a handsome sight at the back of a border, as is fennel, particularly the bronze variety. The advantage of all three of these plants is that they are both herb and spice in one, and having used the leaves you can harvest and store the spicy seeds for cooking. Put chives next to your roses to help their flowering, and try out the other ideas for companion planting mentioned separately under each herb.

For the town dweller herbs are also rewarding since they can be grown in pots indoors, or in tubs and window boxes out of doors. They do enjoy a sunny position and good drainage, but once those requirements are fulfilled nothing will stop them from flourishing. You can plant your herbs either from seed, from cuttings or young plants, or from root runners. They are not expensive, and the speed with which the garden grows is a good return for your outlay. Herbs bring colour and scent to the simplest of gardens, and make an aromatic nosegay throughout the growing year.

Cooking with herbs and other uses

Cooking with herbs is an extension of the pleasures of herb gardening, gathering these sweet-smelling plants from the garden during the summer months for their individual taste and aromas. Apart from being delicious in the pot or the salad bowl, they make delightful posies for the table, either in flower or just using the leaves with all their differing greens.

Herbs have their place in the greatest of the world's gastronomic dishes, from east and west, north and south. Each one has its entirely individual flavour, and they are immensely versatile. They are a joy to cook with as they give an indefinable and special touch to whatever they are mixed with, and fill the kitchen with mouth-watering smells as they are either chopped or cooked.

Some herbs are better used fresh than dried. The best herbs to use fresh are basil, borage, coriander, dill, fennel, tarragon, lovage, chives, tansy and parsley. Some herbs are as good dried as fresh – marigold, marjoram, mint, rosemary, sage and thyme – so these herbs can give the cook pleasure all the year round.

In general, dried herbs are far stronger than fresh ones so smaller quantities are needed in cooking. Dried bay for instance is better than fresh – it is stronger as well as more aromatic. Certainly some herbs dry better than others, and a few are better dried than fresh. Of these, bay, rosemary, sage and thyme are good examples, and coriander and fennel seeds retain the flavour of the leaves (best fresh), and store extremely well.

Herbs are at their most aromatic just before they come into flower, when their essential oil is at its strongest. This is the time to harvest them for drying because they will retain their maximum scent and flavour. Pick them on a dry morning, sunny if possible, just after the dew has dried on them but before the oils in the top shoots have had a chance to dry out. Lay them on paper to dry and put them either on to a sunny windowsill, on top of the boiler, in an airing cupboard, or hang them in bunches in the attic or garage. Fleshier leaves like those of sage will dry out eventually in a very slow oven. When the leaves are so completely dry that they are brittle pull them off the stalks and put them into dark glass containers. If you store them in clear glass, keep them in a dark place because herbs lose their pungency far more rapidly if they are exposed to the light. It is best to replace them every year as they tend to lose their fragrance after long periods of storage.

Herbs have found their way into a wide variety of other uses in everyday life. Some are good insect and moth-repellents, particularly tansy and rue which have rancid, bitter scents. Others keep flies away effectively, or keep pests at bay both in the house and in the garden. This quality led to their use historically as strewing herbs, when branches of aromatic herbs were thrown over the floors of dining halls or public places to disguise smells and to combat disease. So great, it was believed, were the antiseptic properties of herbs that they would even fend off the plague, and people carried nosegays or even had nosebags of herbs and spices tied to their faces to keep infection at bay.

From the eighteenth century onwards, after a severe outbreak of gaol fever in London which caused the death of the Lord Mayor and two judges, the law courts were regularly strewn with herbs, traditionally rosemary, chamomile and mint, to protect the judiciary from being further infected by the men in the dock. The judges were given posies of herbs to carry, a custom which lingers today when the Lord Mayor attends the first two days of each session at the Old Bailey every month from May to September. Now he or she carries a bunch of flowers in season.

'Strewings' are still scattered from Midsummer to Michaelmas at the ceremonial election of the sheriffs of the City of London, and on

September 29 each year, at the election of the Lord Mayor, the aldermen of the City carry posies of herbs and flowers, and the Lord Mayor himself is presented with a nosegay by the Keeper of the Guildhall. The dais of the Guildhall and all the adjacent Livery Halls are strewn with chamomile flowers, mint, and chopped rose petals.

Dried herbs have found their way into aromatic sachets to sweeten rooms, and in Edwardian England ladies made small silk bags containing bergamot, lemon verbena, scented geranium, thyme, mint, lavender, rosemary and southernwood. These were hung on the backs of chairs to scent the drawing rooms throughout the winter, and likewise elegant houses would have bowls of *pot-pourri* around the rooms, made of dried rose petals and scented geranium leaves to which herbs and spices had been added.

Certain herbs induce drowsiness and have been made into sleep pillows to help insomniacs; others are efficacious for fatigue when steeped in hot bath water, and aching limbs and sore bodies can be relieved in these baths too. These healing qualities have been recognized as effective in the form of tisanes or teas, in the same way as infusions and decoctions (see pages 13 and 14).

The essential oils of herbs are vital ingredients in many cosmetics and so herbs have found their way into beauty care. They are added to skin creams, shampoos, conditioners, lotions, toothpastes, soaps, and perfumes. These oils are also used in exotic and expensive liqueurs and vermouths, whose makers keep their recipes closely-guarded secrets. The magic of herbs indeed!

from The Grete Herball, *1526*

Some lesser herbs

Chervil (*Anthriscus cerefolium*)

A delicious and delicately aromatic herb, chervil is more widely cultivated in France than in the UK – and more's the pity, for this fragrant herb is easy to grow both in open ground in summer and in boxes through the winter. This highly scented plant grows to about 28 inches high, and has pale green, deeply indented leaves, giving the plant a fragile quality. Umbels of white flowers appear in midsummer. A native of the Middle East, chervil prefers light soil, and a certain amount of moisture. Its use is mainly in the kitchen, but it has also been used in country medicine in poultices for painful joints, and in tisanes to ease stomach complaints.

Comfrey (*Symphytum officinale*)

Comfrey gets its generic name from the Greek meaning 'join together', as it was one of the main herbs used in treating fractures. One of its local names is 'knitbone', and the pounded root makes a poultice which can be bound around a fracture and, when dry, holds the bone in place. The leaves have a high food value, containing Vitamin B_{12} and almost 35 per cent protein, the same as that of soya beans. In parts of the world such as Africa it is important as animal feed, and it is also grown as organic compost and mulch.

Comfrey grows from 12–48 inches tall, with lance-shaped hairy leaves and drooping purplish or pink flowers through the summer months. It thrives on rich, wet soils and is often to be found near rivers and streams. The root was used in folk medicine for the treatment of diarrhoea, and of gastric and duodenal ulcers. The leaves were used to cure pleurisy and bronchitis; they are also delicious cooked as a vegetable and used in the same ways as spinach.

French Sorrel (*Rumex scutatus*)

This 'garden sorrel', as it is also called, has a mildly sour, lemony taste and is a valuable member of the herb garden. It is native to Europe and Asia and it is now widely cultivated throughout the world. It likes rich, moist soil, and provides leaf throughout most of the year. It is a perennial which grows to between 14–20 inches tall, and small reddish flowers appear in late summer. The leaves are delicious raw in salads in small amounts, and cooked, make a delicious sauce for fish or eggs. Sorrel contains Vitamin C and oxalic acid, and moderate amounts are diuretic.

Lovage (*Ligusticum scoticum*)

Lovage is also called 'sea parsley', growing as it does by rocky shores, and it was popular with sailors and fishermen suffering from scurvy. It has a high Vitamin C content, and North American Indians used to peel the stems and eat them in order to supplement their diet. It is a tall, handsome garden plant growing about 24 inches tall, bearing yellowish white umbels of flowers in the late summer. It has a strong, individual flavour and is delicious in summer salads and soups – both leaf and stem are edible. The seed can be powdered and used like pepper, and the root can be used to scent a bath – in the old days it was chewed as a tobacco substitute.

Savory, Summer (*Satureja hortensis*)

Summer savory is a highly aromatic herb and has been used to flavour food for over 2,000 years. It is delicious both in salads and in cooked foods. Savory is a native of the eastern Mediterranean, and the Italians have cultivated it since the ninth century. It grows on chalky soils to about 12–16 inches, with pale pink, lilac or white flowers. Its slim spear-shaped leaves contain a pungent essential oil which is used to flavour salami. Savory has its medicinal uses, too – it is powerfully antiseptic and was used in the old days to cure gastric complaints and to stimulate the appetite. So stimulating was it that some herbalists held that it was an aphrodisiac!

Savory, Winter (*Satureja montana*)

Winter savory has much the same properties as summer savory, but its flavour is coarser and stronger. It gets its name from being a hardier plant which can provide leaf throughout the year in warmer climates than our own. It is a perennial evergreen and also called mountain savory. Shrubby, it grows from between 4–16 inches, in a compact bush, and bears white or pink flowers in spikes from early to late summer.

Balm

Name

Balm's generic name *melissa* means a beé, and until the fifteenth century it was known either as *mellissophylon*, Greek for 'bee-leaf', or *apiastrum*, Latin for 'bee-plant'. Balm is an abbreviation of balsam, after its sweet lemony scent. Local names are Lemon Balm, Common Balm and Bee Balm.

History

In ancient Greece, balm was the chief of the sweet oils used in perfumery and one of the sacred herbs in the Temple of Diana. Because of its sweetness the Greeks used it to make lovers' chaplets, intertwining it amongst other small flowers.

Balm – the bee-leaf or bee-plant – has been used to attract bees for centuries. It used to be planted around orchards and around vegetable plots to encourage pollination. During the seventeenth and eighteenth centuries particularly, balm was used by apiarists to make bees stay in their hives, and today bee keepers still find that rubbing the inside of a hive with a handful of lemon balm will make a new swarm of bees eager to stay, and may even attract another swarm. This age-old trick was known to Pliny in the first century AD, here translated by Gerard: 'Bees are delighted with this herbe above all others. . . . When they are straied away, they do find their way home againe by it.'

Melissa officinalis
Labiatae

27

Folklore

- Give balm leaves to cows to increase their flow of milk.

- Balm is 'good against a surfeit of mushrooms'.

- Balm is the 'scholars' herb'. In the past, balm tea was given to students to clear their heads and sharpen both memory and understanding.

- Wearing balm leaves in a sachet next to your heart will make you attractive, happy and healthy.

- In the 'Language of Flowers' balm stands for 'joking', because it makes people cheerful and merry, and composes even the nervous. This is backed up by John Evelyn, the seventeenth-century diarist, who alludes to its 'cordial and exhilarating effect'.

Folk medicine

Balm is principally renowned for being a relaxant and good for the heart – literally a 'cordial'. The Arabs described it in early medicine as 'gladdening', because it revitalized the spirits and banished melancholy. It was used in country medicine for anxiety and depression and to calm palpitations of the heart, so effectively that Hippocrates included it in his 400 simples. Today it is still marketed as a sedative and tonic tea which, according to legend, contains the formula for longevity!

Thomas Coghan, a sixteenth-century Oxford don, wrote: 'It is an herbe greatly to be esteemed of students, for by a special property it driveth away heaviness of mind, sharpeneth the understanding and encreaseth memory.' Evelyn agreed: 'Balm is sovereign for the brain, strengthening the memory and powerfully chasing away melancholy.' And look at all the claims made for Eau de Carmes on the next page.

The essential oil of balm contains citronella and so it has been used as a wound-herb. Pliny described its staunching properties, and Gerard found that 'the juice of balm glueth together greene wounds'. Dioscorides prescribed it for the bites of mad dogs, and as a cure for toothache. And

there is an old folk remedy for boils: 'To ripen and break a boil; bruise a handful of balm, boil it in a little linseed oil and lay it warm on the place.'

Eau de Carmes

Carmelite water, an early version of Eau de Cologne which was used originally for medicinal purposes, was a spirit distilled from balm leaves with lemon, nutmeg, cloves and coriander. It was first made by the nuns of the Abbey of St Just near Paris in 1379, and was prescribed for nervous headaches. In 1611 its manufacture was started in the pharmacy of Carmelite monks in Paris, and it became very popular during the seventeenth century. It was used in the treatment of neuralgia, and taken to restore *joie de vivre* in even the most melancholy. The Holy Roman Emperor, Charles V (1500–58), used it daily in his bath and inhaled it on a handkerchief to refresh and preserve his intellect! Not only was it believed to cure baldness and renew youth, it was also thought to confer longevity: 'An essence of Balm, given in Canary wine, every morning will renew youth, strengthen the brain, relieve languishing nature and prevent baldness', says the *London Dispensatory* of 1692.

Louis XVI was the last surviving sovereign to grant the monks a patent for the manufacture of Eau de Carmes. After 1780 the College of Pharmacy demanded payment of £40 a year from them, and when monastic orders were suppressed in 1781, and their property confiscated, forty-five Carmelites of the monastery of Van Girard formed themselves into a company to produce the balm water. The last survivor, Brother Paradise, died in 1831, but his formula still survives in the French Codex.

Cooking with balm and other uses

Because of its reputed merry-making properties, balm is a traditional garnish for wine cups and cold summer drinks. It has always been an important ingredient of Chartreuse and Benedictine. Fresh lemon balm can be used in some recipes instead of lemon or lemon grass, and

chopped, the leaves contribute flavour to salads, sauces for fish, soups, and stuffings. Dried lemon balm is much used in *pot-pourri*, herb pillows and sachets, and it was widely used as a strewing herb in the old days.

The leaf is a good remedy for insect bites – just rubbing it into the spot will relieve the pain. Balm is also a soothing herb, so you can put a sprig of it in your bath for a sedative and relaxing soak.

Growing balm

Balm is a native of Southern Europe and the Mediterranean, and a cousin of sage and lavender. It was probably introduced into Britain by the Romans, and during the Middle Ages it was widely cultivated north of the Alps in monastery gardens. Around the Mediterranean it has been grown horticulturally and commercially for more than 2,000 years, principally as a bee-plant.

Balm grows happily in rich soil that is moist and well-drained. It likes plenty of sun and a little shade. Growing to about 2 feet tall, it flowers from June to August with small whitish flowers which are sometimes tinged with pink and yellow. The leaves are the same shape as spearmint and are soft to the touch. It has square, hairy stems.

Balm is easy to cultivate as it spreads rapidly by root runners, and seeds itself freely. To start it off, sow seed in the late spring, or divide roots in the autumn or early spring. It is a perennial which dies right back in the winter and is susceptible to frost, so it is advisable to protect the roots in a hard winter. As it is so attractive to bees, balm is a useful plant to grow near fruit trees – to encourage pollination.

Basil

Name

'Basil' is the Greek for king, so perhaps the herb was given its name by people who thought it fine enough for a king, a royal herb with its powerful scent and flavour. In ancient times basil was used as a royal unguent or medicine. Another version has it that basil got its name from the monstrous basilisk, creature of fable.

Commonly known as Sweet Basil, its generic name *Ocimum* comes from the Greek *ozo*, smell.

History

In India, basil is venerated and revered as sacred to the gods, and even worshipped as a deity itself, invoked to protect all parts of the body. Yet it is an ambivalent herb. Sacred as it is, it is also dedicated to the Evil One. In some aspects a herb of happiness, it is also a funeral plant. Dear to women and lovers because of its scent, it is at the same time an emblem of hatred. And whilst it can harbour and even propagate scorpions (see **Folklore**), it is also the antidote to their stings. Culpeper sums it up: 'This is the herb which all authors are together by the ears about, and rail at one another like lawyers.'

In Tudor times a miniature basil plant in a pot was commonly presented to visitors as they left, and basil plants were considered favour gifts by famous ladies to their guests. Farmers' wives often gave gifts of a

Ocimum basilicum
Labiatae

31

pot of basil to their friends, both for cooking with and to keep flies away.

The Italian herbalist, Mattioli (1501–77), wrote: 'There are few gardens, indoors or out, that are not full of basil grown in wooden boxes or clay pots ... It is good for the hart and for the head. The seede cureth the infirmities of the hart, taketh away sorrowfulnesses which cometh of melancholie, and maketh a man merrie and glad.'

Folklore

● Every good Hindu goes to his final rest with a basil leaf on his breast: this is his passport to Paradise.

● Hindus believe that good fortune awaits those who build their houses on a spot where basil has grown freely, and there is no forgiveness in this world or the next for anyone who wilfully uproots it.

● The Greeks said that when you sow basil the act should be accompanied by abuse, without which the herb would not flourish. Pliny also said that it thrived best when sown with cursing and railing. To the French, *semer le basilic* means to slander someone.

● Basil became a symbol of hatred because poverty is sometimes represented by the figure of a female covered in rags seated by a pot of basil.

● In the West, basil is a symbol of fertility. Boccaccio, the fourteenth-century poet and scholar (1313–75), tells the story of Isabella, whose tears watered the pot of basil in which was buried the head of her murdered lover. In Persia – and this was probably known to Boccaccio – basil was planted on graves.

● To dream of basil means grief and misfortune.

● In Italy, the heart-shaped leaves of basil are love tokens. If a girl accepts a sprig of basil from her lover she will fall in love with him immediately.

● In Italy, a pot of basil in the window is a sign that a girl is expecting her lover.

- In Crete, basil is sown in pots as a love plant.
- In the West, basil was believed to have sovereign power over witches.
- In the Middle Ages, it was believed that a sprig of basil laid under a pot would breed a scorpion, and that when the basil was closely smelled it would breed a scorpion in the brain, 'and after long and vehement pain he dies thereof'. Yet basil seeds are thought to cure the bites of scorpions.

Folk medicine

Basil is basically a tranquillizer and sedative. In folk medicine it has been used dried and in the form of snuff to ease nervous headaches and anxiety, and an infusion prescribed to relieve stomach cramps and sickness. Basil is a good digestive, stimulating the appetite as well as relieving constipation. However it is hard to believe Dodoens, who said that 'a woman in labour, if she but hold in her hand a root of this herb together with the feather of a swallow shall be delivered without pain.' Modern aromatherapists recommend basil for menstrual cycle problems and the menopause.

Like borage and balm, basil is meant to be a cheering herb. To quote Gerard, 'Basil is good for the heart ... It taketh away sorrowfulness, which commeth of melancholy and maketh a man merry and glad.' Doctors of his time would prescribe basil for 'cheering the spirit and restoring the humours that compose the body'.

Cooking with basil and other uses

With basil then I will begin,
Whose scent is wondrous pleasing.

John Dryden (1631–1700)

Above all, basil's usefulness lies in its sweet scent. Today it is cultivated commercially in California for its aromatic essential oil, which is used in

perfumery. In the past it was used as a strewing herb and as a herb to keep flies away, still one of its principal uses in present-day Spain and Greece.

Basil is one of the great culinary herbs, with a unique flavour that develops with cooking. Its essential oil contains estragol, which is also present in tarragon, although the two herbs are quite distinctive. Nutritionally speaking, basil contains all the minerals and Vitamin B. It is wonderful in sauces, particularly in *pistou* (basil, garlic and Parmesan) which, in the Provençal dialect, has become synonymous with basil. Its most famous marriage is again with garlic, in the Italian *pesto* (a basil, garlic and pine kernel sauce for pasta). Basil enhances fish and chicken dishes, and is supremely delicious with tomatoes, whether cooked or in salads or even sandwiches. It is also excellent with egg dishes and mushrooms. Traditionally, basil has been used as a flavouring for turtle soup, and was an ingredient in the renowned Fetter Lane sausages of the nineteenth century.

Growing basil

Basil is delicate; it is used to hot climates and cannot tolerate frost. In Northern conditions it flourishes best in a greenhouse, or at the very least in a sunny sheltered position. It needs light, well-drained soil or compost and likes to be well-watered in dry weather. Sow basil seeds indoors in March or April, and this aromatic annual will grow to between 1–2 feet tall, whereas bush basil, of which there is a lemon-scented variety, grows only 6–12 inches high. Basil is rarely found in the wild, but is cultivated principally as a culinary herb. As it grows, nip out the flowers and shoots to use in cooking and to encourage further growth. Like balm, basil attracts bees, so it is a good plant to grow near fruit trees.

A fable of companion planting
The basilisk was the fabulous king of serpents said to be hatched by a snake from the egg of a cock. It advanced almost upright with its crowned

head reared, and would kill anyone on whom it fixed its gaze. Edmund Spenser (1552–99) describes it in 'The Faerie Queene':

> *The Basiliske*
> *From powerful eyes close venim doth convey*
> *Into the looker's heart, and killeth farre away.*

The myth goes that only a weasel was cunning enough to combat the basilisk. This he did by eating rue, and thus fortified he attacked and killed the monster. It is true that rue and basil will not flourish in the same garden; the sweetest herb has an antipathy to the bitterest.

> *Fine basil desireth it may be her lot*
> *To grow as a gelliflower, trim in a pot;*
> *That ladies and gentles, to whom ye do serve,*
> *May help her, as needeth, poor life to preserve.*

Thomas Tusser (c.1520–80)

Bay

Name

Laurus nobilis is a noble tree, tree of oracles and victories. *Laurus* means triumph or victory; *nobilis* means noble. Bay is also commonly known as Sweet Bay and Sweet Laurel.

> *The Gods, that mortal beauty chase,*
> *Still in a tree did end their race.*
> *Apollo hunted Daphne so,*
> *Only that she might Laurel grow.*
>
> *An Horatian Ode*, Andrew Marvell (1521–78)

History

The bay tree was sacred to Apollo, god of music and poetry, prophecy and healing, who was often depicted as the perfection of youthful manhood. It was also dedicated to Aesculapius, god of medicine, because it was regarded by the ancient Greeks as a panacea of all ailments: Aesculapius' statue was traditionally crowned with a wreath of sweet bay. The bay tree was both useful and propitious, protective and healing, and the Greeks believed that the man who carried a laurel branch had no need to fear either poison or sorcery. Roman emperors were known to wear sprigs of laurel during a storm to protect them from lightning, and from misfortune

Laurus nobilis
Lauraceae

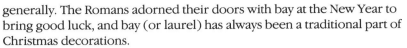

generally. The Romans adorned their doors with bay at the New Year to bring good luck, and bay (or laurel) has always been a traditional part of Christmas decorations.

Bay became a symbol of eternity not just because of its evergreen leaves but because for a long while after they are cut, the leaves do not wither or fall from the branch. So bay was carried at funerals as a symbol of the Resurrection. Thus the decay of a bay tree came to be a bad omen; before the death of Nero, it was said that all the bay trees in Rome withered at the root even though it was a mild winter. Shakespeare knew of this myth and quoted it in *Macbeth*;

> *Tis thought the king is dead: we will not stay,*
> *The bay trees in our country are all withered.*

Bay is thought to inspire visions and the leaves are thought to be slightly intoxicating: the priestess of Apollo at Delphi chewed bay leaves for inspiration when consulted as the Oracle. It was traditional for diviners to wear a laurel wreath, and a branch of laurel was thought to give prophets the gifts of insight and foresight. It even inspired creativity: John Evelyn wrote that 'it greatly composed the phansy, and did facilitate true visions . . . and specifically to inspire a poetic fury'.

Above all, bay represents glory. The winner of the Pythian Games in ancient Greece was crowned with a wreath of laurel, or sometimes beech. To the Romans, a laurel wreath became a symbol of the highest achievement: The palace gates of the Caesars were decorated with laurel, and despatches to the Senate announcing victory in battle were wrapped in bay leaves. More recently the mail coaches which carried the news of the victory at Waterloo were festooned with laurel branches.

The word 'laurels' has become synonymous with success. The highest honour a Greek poet or warrior could receive was a garland of fruiting laurel, and we still crown our 'poet laureate' today. It was tradition, also, to crown young doctors with berried laurel, *bacca lauri*, hence the *Baccalaureate*. This, in its turn, is the derivation of the term 'bachelor' of a subject – not an unmarried man but a standard of achievement. The term describes his 'laurels' rather than his condition!

Folklore

* *If you hear fire crack loud with bay*
  Much kindness soon shall come your way.

• Throw bay leaves on to the fire, and if they crackle noisily it is a sign of good luck to come. If they burn silently the omens are bad.

• Burning bay leaves will bring back a departed or errant lover, because of the delicious smell.

• A bay tree drives away ghosts, witches and evils.

• A bay tree will never be struck by lightning, so it offers protection in a storm.

• A laurel branch over the door of someone who is sick will protect him from death, avert the plague and drive out evil spirits.

• If two lovers pick a bay twig and break it in two, and each keeps his own half, then they will remain faithful to each other.

• Bay trees induce sleep and a leaf under your pillow at night will give you pleasant dreams, and also enable you to foresee events in your dreams.

• Put two bay leaves under your pillow on St Valentine's night and you will dream of love and be married within the year if you recite this ditty;

> *St Valentine, be kind to me,*
> *In my dreams let me my true love see.*

• If a bay tree dies in the garden, it means that there will be a death in the family.

Cooking with bay and other uses

Bay's culinary use is the flavouring of stocks, meat dishes, stews and casseroles. It is a vital ingredient of a *bouquet garni* and it also lends a delicious flavour to barbecued foods.

Two or three bay leaves in a hot bath will relieve aching limbs and

help tone up the body, and if you are stung by a serpent Culpeper advises that 'the berries are very effectual against all poisons of venomous creatures, as also against the pestilence and other infectious diseases'.

Because of its exquisite aroma, bay was used as incense by the ancient Greeks in their great temples, and the sweet smell of burning bay was often used in the old days to scent the air in the house, 'to expel corrupt and contagious air in the buttery, the cellar, the kitchen, the larder house'. Today, just a sprig of bay hung in the room acts as an freshener.

Growing bay

Bay is a native of Northern Asia, but is now distributed throughout Europe and the Mediterranean. It is frequently seen flourishing in towns and cities as it is highly resistant to pollution. It is a member of the laurel family, evergreen shrubs which are spread over a number of genera and species, for example the cherry laurel, Japanese laurel and daphne (spurge laurel).

Bay is a closely-branched shrub which can grow up to 20 feet in height, with thick evergreen leaves containing glands which give off a rich, sweet smell when the leaf is crushed. It bears yellowish-green flowers in May and June, male and female on different trees, and green berries which blacken as they ripen in October. Naturally pyramid shaped, bay can withstand training and heavy clipping, and has often been used decoratively in formal gardens. It flourishes in medium to light soils and needs a sunny but sheltered position as it dislikes frost and may not survive a very hard winter.

Bergamot

Name

Bergamot's generic name *Monarda* comes from Dr Nicholas Monardes, a Spanish physician whose book *Joyful News out of the New Founde World* was translated into English in 1577. Its specific name *didyma* describes its seed pods which separate into two, and also its habit of twin-flowering. It has local names of Bee Balm (coined by the gardener William Robinson in the nineteenth century when he noticed its attraction for bees), and Oswego Tea (because the Oswego tribe on the shores of Lake Ontario made infusions of bergamot for medicinal purposes).

History

Bergamot was introduced into Britain from America by Peter Collinson in 1745, and during the nineteenth century a bergamot plant would often form part of a girl's dowry since the tea made from bergamot was thought to help fertility in young mothers-to-be. Aromatic Oswego tea, made from the leaves of the lemon-scented bergamot, *M. citriodora*, replaced Indian tea in many American households after the Boston Tea Party in 1733 as a protest against the heavy tea duty imposed on the colonies. The distinctive flavour of Earl Grey tea is given by the addition of oil of bergamot, obtained from the like smelling and tasting bergamot orange tree.

Monarda didyma
Labiatae

Folklore

- In Dorset it was thought that if bergamot was brought into the house it would bring sickness and death with it.

Folk medicine

The volatile essential oil of bergamot is related to thymol, so it is good for sore throats, colds and chest complaints. An infusion of the leaves in hot milk makes a sedative nightcap, sweetened with honey if desired, and bergamot tea relieves nausea, flatulence, menstrual pain and headaches.

Cooking with bergamot and other uses

Bergamot leaves are a tasty addition to pork dishes, their slightly minty flavour acting as a foil to rich meats. They are also a fragrant addition to a wine cup. The vivid scarlet of the wild bergamot looks wonderful as a decoration on salads, and the cultivated varieties, too, with their colourful flowers, can be used to garnish cold dishes and soups.

Bergamot produces abundant nectar and is a bee-plant which produces exquisite honey. It is highly aromatic and its essential oil is used in perfumery, and used to be added to hair preparations. It is a favourite in *pot-pourri*, and a simple vase of bergamot flowers can make a dramatic and original arrangement.

In the old days, bergamot was used to perfume starch. A nineteenth-century recipe goes: 'Stand some Bergamot and Lavender petals in Rose water all night and add the perfume so obtained to your starch, which you must make thicker than usual. This will give a nice perfume to linen.'

Growing bergamot

Bergamot is a native of North America and, like its cousin mint, is easily propagated from root division early in the year. Alternatively, it can be grown from seed in the spring. The plant likes a light but rich, moist soil and will not tolerate full sun, preferring shade – in the wild it is found in deciduous woodland. Cut it back in the autumn and replace it every three years or so as it tends to die back in the centre of the clump.

Its dramatic red flowers are pompoms, like fireworks of dazzling scarlet, and smell like the bergamot-oranges after which the plant is named. The wild strain has been cultivated to produce a range of pinks, salmons, magentas, rose-pinks, purples and whites, so it takes its place in the herbaceous border as well as in the herb garden.

Borage

Name

Borage got its name from the Latin *burra*, rough hair or a shaggy garment, affectionately describing its furry leaves. The Celtic word *borrach* means 'glad courage', with which borage has always been associated. Local names include Bee Bread, Cool Tankard and Herb of Gladness, alluding to its three main attributes: a bee-plant, its use in wine cups, and its quality as a 'cheering' herb. In some parts of Britain it is called 'burrage'.

History

When talking of borage this much is clear
That it warms the heart and it brings good cheer.
School of Salerno (11th–12th century)

This couplet sums up borage's reputation as nature's 'happiness' plant. Both flowers and leaves have bedecked wine cups for centuries – principally in the belief that they would raise the spirits and make the most melancholy merry. The ancient Greeks claimed that borage steeped in wine was a sure remedy for depression. Pliny coined a little epithet for it, as quoted by Gerard: 'I, Borage, bring alwaies courage.' Today, it is still a classic addition to a jug of Pimms. So borage instills both happiness and courage, and also, according to John Evelyn, 'sprigs of borage are of known virtue to revive the hypochondriac and cheer the hard student.'

Borago officinalis
Boraginaceae

43

Gerard sings its praises, too: 'Those of our time do use the flowers in salads to exhilarate and make the mind glad. There be also many things made of these used everywhere for the comfort of the heart, for the driving away of sorrow and increasing the joy of the mind.... Syrup made of the floures of Borage comforteth the heart, purgeth melancholy and quieteth the phrenticke and lunaticke person.'

In the 'Language of Flowers' borage stands for bluntness, because its rough appearance is a reminder that bluntness is often accompanied by a good heart.

Folk medicine

Its specific name *officinalis* reveals that borage was recognized by the medical profession of old as an effective medicine. It was used in the treatment of weak hearts and was believed to be good for the blood as it is rich in potassium and the mineral acid nitrate of potash. Alfred the Great certainly knew it as such and referred to it as 'a maker of good blood'. A tisane of borage used to be prescribed for rheumatism and respiratory infections, and cooled a fever as well as calming delirium. It was also said to stimulate the flow of milk in nursing mothers.

In French homoeopathic medicine, a drug derived from borage is still today used to treat fevers and nervous disorders.

Cooking with borage

Borage leaves taste and smell rather like cucumber when bruised. Borage soup not only tastes delicious but its soft green colour looks beautiful, especially with a garnish of one of its brilliant blue flowers floating in the middle of the bowl. Borage leaves make a subtle addition to a summery pea soup, too.

The soft, grey-green, hairy leaves can be cooked as a vegetable, like spinach and lightly buttered – again decorated with its dazzling flowers. In certain areas of Italy, borage, again like spinach, is used as a stuffing for

ravioli. You can also add borage leaves to spring cabbage at the end of the cooking time to give extra flavour. The raw leaves are delicious in salads and sandwiches and they make excellent fritters, cooked in light batter and eaten hot from the pan.

Candied borage flowers make a beautiful garnish for cakes and desserts, and the leaves make a refreshing summer tea.

Growing borage

Borage is a native annual of the Eastern Mediterranean and, once established in the garden, it will seed itself prolifically so long as the soil and drainage conditions are right. Sow seeds in the spring in light, fairly poor soil which is moist but well-drained. Borage grows up to 2 feet high and is one of the beauties of the herb garden with its soft, grey-green leaves covered with downy hairs, and its bright cobalt blue, star-shaped flowers. These flowers have been the inspiration for needlework and tapestries for hundreds of years.

Chamomile

Name

It hath floures wonderfully shynynge yellow and resemblynge the appell of an eye.

William Turner (c.1520–68)

Chamaemelum is the Greek for 'apple on the ground'. To their ancient civilization this herb was an earth-apple, growing low in the fields with a fragrant apple scent. Its common names include Roman Chamomile, Common and Double Chamomile. There are many different species: German Chamomile, *Matricaria recutita*, is also known as Wild Chamomile and gets its generic name from *matrix*, a womb, because chamomile was once used to ease painful menstruation.

Charming abbreviations of the word chamomile have found their way into local names; in Cornwall and Somerset it is Camel and Camil, in Lancashire Cammary, and in Scotland Camovyne.

History

The ancient Egyptians held chamomile in such reverence that they consecrated it to their gods, and it has been used in country folk medicine ever since. It was, however, a fairly rare plant in medieval England, brought into cultivation from the wild in about 1265 and planted in infirmary gardens. King Edward III's wardrobe accounts mention a

Chamaemelon nobile
Compositae

purchase of chamomile, to be used as a clothes freshener.

By the seventeenth century, chamomile was in regular use as a medicinal and beauty herb, and the Pilgrim Fathers took it with them to the New World. In the late nineteenth century it was grown in Mitcham, Surrey, alongside the world-famous Mitcham lavender, purely for medicinal purposes.

Folk medicine

The deep blue oil extracted from chamomile flowers contains azulene, an anti-inflammatory substance, and thus a poultice of chamomile will effectively bring down swellings. As an eye lotion, it soothes and heals, and it also makes a good dressing for insect bites and stings.

Infusions of chamomile alleviate stomach cramps and muscle spasms, colic and painful menstruation. It is also a tonic, mild sedative, and good for a cold as it promotes sweating.

Cooking with chamomile and other uses

Little sprigs of chamomile are a tasty addition to a salad, and give an original flavour to sauces and mayonnaise. Try the leaves chopped up in an *omelette aux fines herbes*, or mix them into a bread dough in the manner of the traditional Provençal bakers. For a touch of elegance at a dinner party fill fingerbowls with chamomile water and orange peel.

Chamomile is added to manzanilla sherry for its apple flavour and scent (*manzanilla* being a Spanish name for the plant), and in the Middle Ages, before the advent of the hop, the whole herb was used in the manufacture of beer.

Chamomile makes an excellent rinse for highlighting blond hair and it is now cultivated for its use in shampoos. When chamomile oil is massaged into the scalp, it gives lustre to lifeless hair. A few drops in the bath will relieve fatigue and give a good night's rest.

Chamomile tea is now widely marketed in tea-bags as a sedative

and tonic tea, and is said to relax the facial muscles and so help erase unlovely lines.

> *Peter was not very well during the evening. His mother put him to bed, and made some camomile tea: 'one table-spoonful to be taken at bed-time'.*   *Peter Rabbit*, Beatrix Potter (1866–1943)

Growing chamomile

Chamomile grows wild in meadows and grass verges and on the edges of woods. It is a native of Southern Europe and thrives on waste ground and poor, sandy soils, surviving the worst of the droughts. It likes light, moist soils and plenty of sun, and you can grow it from seed planted in the spring or propagate it from root runners. It has been harvested in the wild from the earliest times and is now cultivated for its medicinal and cosmetic properties. For herbal teas, the flowers should be gathered just as the petals begin to turn down.

There are about 200 species of chamomile, which include the Lawn Chamomile, which is Roman Chamomile, the German or Wild Chamomile, Corn Chamomile, Stinking Mayweed and Yellow Chamomile.

A chamomile lawn

A lawn of creeping chamomile is a delight, its apple fragrance wafting up as you walk on it. 'The more it is trodden, the more it will spread,' maintains Falstaff in *Henry IV*. Plant it from seed, or with young plants set slightly apart. If you keep it lightly but regularly watered, and mown to about $\frac{1}{2}$ inch high, it will wear as well as grass.

Companion planting

● Chamomile is known as 'the plant's physician', because if it is grown near sickly or unhealthy plants of any kind, they seem to recover their health.

● Chamomile growing near wheat helps it to grow heavy with fuller ears.

Chives

Allium schoenoprasum
Liliaceae

Name

A member of the onion family, *Allium schoenoprasum* is also known as Rush-leek after the Greek *skhoinos*, rush, and *prason*, leek. Allium is the old name for garlic, chives' cousin, possibly derived from the Celtic *all*, meaning pungent.

History and medicine

Although chives were introduced into Britain by the Romans, they were not cultivated here until the Middle Ages. Yet the Chinese grew them 5,000 years ago, and used them not only in cooking but in medicine too, as an antidote to poisoning and as a remedy for bleeding. Since then they have continued to play a small role only in folk medicine because, like all the alliums they are a good antiseptic. Being rich in iron, they are also good for anaemia, and since their action is diuretic they have been used to assist kidney function.

Cooking with chives and other uses

Chives are an excellent appetizer and digestive, and one of the most popular herbs to be used as a garnish. They enhance vegetable dishes, are delicious in omelettes, and versatile in sauces and salads. Chopped

chives in cream cheese or butter are lovely with baked potatoes, and the little bulbs can be pickled in vinegar, like baby onions. The aroma of chives is destroyed with long cooking, so they are best added to hot dishes at the end of the cooking time.

Growing chives

Chives are a hardy perennial plant, found in the wild in a great variety of habitats, from dry rocky places to damp grassland and woodland edges. They are native to cool parts of Europe, and best of all they like a light, rich, damp soil. Sow the seed in April for little clumps in the autumn. Cut right back in the winter, and the following spring the leaves will grow from their cluster of tiny bulblets more thickly than ever. If the leaves go yellow at the top give them some plant food, and lift and divide the clumps every three or four years. Cut the mauve, ball-like, flowers throughout the summer to keep the flavour in the leaves – they are very pretty in a vase of mixed flowers and, like all the allium family, dry well for dried flower arrangements.

Chinese chives, *A. tuberosum*, have broader leaves, which are flat and solid and have a coarser flavour. Its flowers are dazzling white balls of stars which attract clouds of butterflies until late in the summer.

Companion planting

- Grow chives next to roses and they will not succumb to black spot.
- Chives growing next to carrots discourage carrot-fly.
- Chives next to apple trees prevent apple scab.
- An infusion of chives is a good spray for mildew on gooseberries.

Coriander

Name

Coriander gets its name from the Greek *koris*, a bed-bug, because of its unpleasant smell when very young, which is similar to the smell of bed-bugs! *Sativum* means cultivated. Local names include Chinese Parsley, after its common use in Oriental cookery, and Dizzicorn, because it was thought that, crushed and inhaled, the aroma of fresh coriander will reduce dizziness.

History

Coriander is herb and spice rolled into one, and may well be man's oldest flavouring. Five thousand years before Christ it was being used in Oriental cooking, and it is one of the earliest plants to be cultivated by man for both its leaf and seed. It is mentioned as a love-potion in the *Arabian Nights* and also finds a place in Assurbanipal's library of medical works.

In the Bible, coriander is one of the five plants designated as bitter herbs, ordained by God to be eaten by the Jews at the feast of the Passover. Manna was described thus in *Numbers* XI 7: 'It was like coriander seed, white; and the taste of it was like wafers made with honey.'

In Pliny's day the best coriander seed was said to come from Egypt. The Romans used it to flavour bread, and the Greeks used it in the cooking of vegetables, in a traditional way which is with us still – *à la Grecque*, a classic method of flavouring dishes with coriander seeds.

Coriandrum sativum
Umbelliferae

Folklore

- If an expectant mother, acting on the advice of the Wise Woman, ate quince and coriander seed, her child, it was promised, would be ingenious and witty.

- The Chinese have a saying that coriander confers immortality on those who eat it.

Folk medicine

Coriander was one of the simples of Hippocrates, and over the centuries it has been used as a medicine to soothe the stomach and prevent griping. Chewing the seed stimulates the secretion of gastric juices, and coriander was still listed in the British Pharmacopoeia at the beginning of this century. Coriander water was a country remedy for 'windy colic', and Arab women took it to ease labour pains. So coriander was a herb to relieve internal pain, a stomach herb and a mild stimulant.

Herbalists claimed that coriander was narcotic, and the botanist William Turner reported that the seeds, 'if taken oute of measure, it doth trouble a manne's witte, with great jeopardye of madnes'. Albertus Magnus's *Boke of Secretes* tells us that coriander is aphrodisiac if picked in the last quarter of the moon, and Robert Turner, writing in the seventeenth century in his *British Physician*, says that the powder of seeds taken in wine stimulates the passions.

Coriander was used as a cure for St Anthony's Fire, or ergotism, and yet Gerard claimed that the juice from the leaves 'taken in the quantity of four dragmes, killeth and poisoneth the body'.

Cooking with coriander and other uses

Coriander has always been particularly popular in Eastern cookery, both the leaf and the seed giving their distinctive flavours to Indian, Chinese

and Indonesian dishes. Peruvians are so fond of the scent and taste of coriander that it is used in almost all their dishes. It almost merits a cookery book of its own!

The leaves of coriander give a superlative flavour to sauces and soups, are widely used as a garnish in Indian food, and are delicious in salads. Combined with ginger and garlic, coriander is an essential herb in great Oriental dishes of fish, curries, chutneys, and in vegetable recipes.

The seeds are used as a spice in baking breads, cakes and biscuits, in Scandinavian pastries, in liqueur manufacture and also in confectionery. In Germany, they are used to flavour sausages and frankfurters. Slightly crushed, they add a new dimension to braised vegetables like chicory and celery, are lovely with beetroot, and make a happy marriage with courgettes and cauliflower. Mushrooms *à la Grecque* are world-famous and rely heavily on coriander seed for their flavour. The root of coriander is a flavouring peculiar to Thai cuisine.

Coriander was used as a beauty herb, especially for the skin. The water would tone down a florid complexion, and many Eastern recipes recommend it to achieve a desirable pallor. In the Middle Ages it was used to clear a spotty face.

Coriander is a highly aromatic herb, much loved by bees, and its seeds, an ingredient of Eau de Carmes (see page 29), can be added to *pot-pourri*. So strong is their scent that they could be used as a preservative too, and in the old days they were rubbed into meat along with cumin and vinegar to keep it fresh in warm weather.

The *Child's Guide* of 1840 mentions its use by distillers and druggists, and in 1979 coriander was still being cultivated in Essex for its use in the manufacture of gin.

Growing coriander

Coriander is a native of the Eastern Mediterranean, found growing in the regions of the Bosphorus and the Dardanelles. It has spread as a weed throughout Europe and was brought to Britain by the Romans, later to be

grown in monastery gardens. It can be found growing wild in the South-East, probably as a garden escape.

Coriander needs a light, rich soil and full sun, and will grow well in pots and window boxes so long as they are well-drained. Sow the seed in the late spring, in drills about 1 inch deep – and be patient, for germination can be slow. Thin out when the plants are several inches tall. At this stage they will smell very nasty, but as the plants mature they develop their pleasantly aromatic scent.

Coriander is an annual, with bright green, deeply-indented leaves which are feathery at the top of the plant and more rounded further down. It flowers in June and July with purplish-white umbels of flowers which later set the seed which has made coriander famous. It is now widely cultivated in the West, in Europe, Morocco and the United States.

Companion planting

- Coriander, dill, mallow, chervil, anise and caraway all benefit from growing near to one another, and fruit well when they are neighbours.

- Don't plant coriander near to fennel as it hinders the formation of fennel seed.

Dill

Anethum graveolens
Umbelliferae

Name

Dill's generic name *Anethum* is the Latin name for fennel, to which dill is so similar, and *graveolens* means strong-smelling. It gets its common name, dill, from the Anglo-Saxon *dillan*, meaning to lull or soothe, after the soothing quality of dill water on the stomach. It is commonly known as Dill-weed and Dill-seed.

History

Dill leaves have been used as a herb, and the seed as a spice, from the earliest times. Like coriander and fennel it is a doubly useful plant, providing a harvest throughout the growing season, with its leaves as delicious as its seeds. It is mentioned in the Bible, in Egyptian texts, and was recommended by Greek and Roman physicians. It was under cultivation in England by 1570, and the Pilgrim Fathers took it with them to America where it thrived, there to become known as 'meetin' seed', because dill seeds were given to children to chew during long Sunday sermons.

Folklore

● A potent witches' herb, dill was used in charms and spells.

- Also, ambivalently, powerful against witches, it was hung over doors and windows as a protection against the Evil Eye, as in this traditional rhyme:

    Vervain and Dill
    Hinder witches from their will.

- Dill is a plant of good omen, worn for luck – especially by English country brides who used to wear a sprig of dill on their wedding day.

Folk medicine

Dill is a constituent of gripe water and is still often used in children's medicines, since it is good for minor digestive problems and even hiccups. Galen wrote that 'dill procureth sleep, wherefore garlands of Dill are worn at feasts', and today dill tea is still recommended for a good night's sleep. It is astringent, and has been used in folk medicine as an external application for piles. According to Pythagoras, an epileptic fit could be prevented if a stem of dill were held in the left hand!

Cooking with dill and other uses

Dill is a characteristic flavouring of Scandinavian cooking – particularly in *gravlax* – and is also popular in Turkey and Russia. It gives a beautiful taste to many other marinated fish such as herring fillets, and is used in pickling baby cucumbers or gherkins (the dill pickles of the USA). Dill also makes an excellent vinegar. Dill seeds give their caraway taste to cakes and pastries which, traditionally, were often served up after a rich meal to settle the stomach.

The leaves, with a gentler and more aniseed flavour than the seeds, add subtlety to soups, sauces and fish dishes, and in Poland they cook new potatoes and peas with dill weed in much the same way that we use mint. The herb goes very well with all kinds of vegetables – mushrooms in cream with dill, on toast, makes a lovely supper dish served with a refreshing salad of cucumber, fresh dill and lemon juice. Dill butter is

delicious on baked potatoes, with grilled steak, or tossed with new potatoes or baby carrots. Spread dill butter on hot French bread, or mix chopped dill into cream cheese to make sandwiches. Dill seed is often used to flavour *sauerkraut* and can be sprinkled on top of a bread dough instead of poppy or sesame seeds.

Dill's pleasant aroma is used to perfume soap, and the plant is popular with bees. It appears to be a favourite of cats, too – mine ignores the catmint and makes its summer camp among the dill!

Growing dill

Dill is native to Southern Europe and the USSR, an annual or biennial member of the same family as parsley, and is now widely cultivated in Europe, India and North America. It grows about 3 feet tall and has feathery leaves growing from a single stalk, and large yellow umbels of clustered flowers at midsummer. Although it will tolerate most soils, it prefers a warm position where it will often self-seed. The best way to grow it is to sow the seeds in drills in the spring.

Companion planting

● Dill grows well next to cabbages, but not with carrots.

● Don't plant dill near fennel as they may cross-fertilize. This weakens the strain and the end product will have neither the flavour nor scent of either herb.

● Dill grows well near coriander, chervil and mallow, as Pliny knew: 'Coriander, Dill, Mallow, Herb Patience and Chervil love for companie for to be set or sowne together.'

Fennel

Name

Fennel's name has derived from the Old English *fenkel*, and its generic name *Foeniculum* means little hay (when dried the leaves resemble very fine hay). *Vulgare* means common. It is also known as Sweet Fennel, and in parts of England and Scotland has won the charming local name of Finkle.

History

The ancient Greeks knew and appreciated fennel, and they turned it into a symbol of success by crowning the winners of their Olympic games with wreaths of fennel. They called it *marathon*, either in reference to their great victory at Marathon over the Persians in 490 BC, or possibly after the word *maraino*, to grow thin – they held that fennel was the herb for slimmers, that it keeps the body from putting on fat. Its aniseed taste certainly diminishes the appetite and, because it allays hunger pangs, it was one of the herbs allowed on fasting days – with the advantage that it was considered a sacred herb as well.

In the 'Language of Flowers' fennel came to stand for strength, because gladiators apparently mixed it with their food to build up their strength. Greek athletes were also known to take it for stamina as well as for courage, and as a guard against becoming overweight.

Introduced to Britain by the Romans, fennel became a popular

Foeniculum vulgare
Umbelliferae

herb in the Middle Ages, and contemporary accounts show that in the thirteenth century fennel was bought for three pence a pound. In 1282, during the reign of Edward I, eight and a half pounds of fennel was a month's supply for the royal household.

Like dill seeds, fennel seeds were called 'meetin' seeds' by the non-conformists of the New World, chewed to sustain them through interminable Sunday sermons.

Folklore

● The ancient Greeks believed that Prometheus concealed the fire of the sun in a hollow stalk and brought it down to earth from heaven for the human race. A closely related myth relates that knowledge came to man from Olympus in the form of a fiery coal contained in a fennel stalk.

● Fennel was strewn across the pathway of a newly-married couple in classical times.

● Fennel is a protective herb. It wards off witchcraft and is dedicated to St John the Baptist. It was woven into garlands which were hung over doorways on the eve of June 24, his feast, and Midsummer's Day.

● Sprigs of fennel hung from the rafters would drive evil spirits out of a house.

● Pliny wrote that serpents love fennel because it rejuvenates them, causing them to cast off their old skins. It also restores their eyesight if it is failing!

● There are two country proverbs about fennel: one says, 'He who sees Fennel and gathers it not is not a man but a Devil'; the other, 'To sow fennel is to sow sorrow.'

Folk medicine

Fennel was one of the simples of Hippocrates, and for centuries was used

in slimming diets because its anise flavour stops hunger pangs. It is also a constituent, like dill, of gripe-water since it relieves cramps. *The Englishman's Doctor* of 1608 quotes this couplet:

In fennel seed this vertue you shall find,
Foorth your lower parts to drive the winde.

Culpeper said that fennel was good for mushroom poisoning, and that it 'takes away the loathings which often times happen to the stomachs of the sick and feverish persons'. Fennel also had a traditional country reputation for strengthening the eyesight, and infusions of fennel seeds were used in an eyewash. Gerard claimed that the seed, 'drunke for certaine dayes together, fasting, preserveth the eyesight'.

Cooking with fennel and other uses

Fennel has featured in cookery for 2,000 years, with its succulent stem, seeds and leaves which are all delicious. It is the best herb of all for fish, with a unique anise flavour, and is used extensively in Mediterranean cookery. A classic recipe for sea bass with fennel, *loup de mer au fenouil*, describes how the fish is grilled and then flamed in brandy on a bed of dried fennel. The stems can be boiled and eaten like asparagus, and both the peeled and raw stems and the leaves are delicious in salads, or finely chopped and sprinkled over cooked eggs. Fennel goes well with potatoes and in cheese dishes, and the seeds are often put on bread or in crackers. The Elizabethans sugared the seeds, and Parkinson wrote that 'Fennell is of great use to trim up and strowe upon fish, as also to boyle or put among fish of divers sorts, cowcumbers pickled and other fruits also.' Fennel vinegar makes a tasty vinaigrette.

Try adding fennel seed to an apple pie – it makes an original and appetizing difference. The seeds are also added to curry, and give their unique flavour to a particular variety of Italian sausage.

All parts of the fennel plant are aromatic, but the highest concentration of oil is in the seed. This has been much used in perfumery

and in the manufacture of liqueurs, and you can chew fennel seed as a breath-sweetener. Fennel leaves were popular as a strewing herb.

Growing fennel

Fennel is a native of the Mediterranean, of Southern Europe and Asia Minor, and is now cultivated in the United States, Great Britain and temperate Eurasia. A hardy perennial, fennel will grow on poor soils so long as it is well-drained – it has an aversion to heavy clay. It enjoys a sunny position, and once established needs to be divided every three to four years. A close relative which is now grown commercially and horticulturally – bronze fennel is a handsome plant in a herbaceous border – Florence fennel or finocchio is cultivated for its swollen root which makes a delicious side vegetable steamed and served with butter, and a crunchy addition to a salad. It feathery leaves can also be used as flavouring.

Fennel can grow up to 8 feet tall, and has flat umbels of small yellow flower clusters in the summer.

Companion planting

• Do not plant fennel next to dill as they are closely related and cross-pollination may occur, causing the flavours to mingle.

• Do not grow fennel near coriander or caraway, dwarf beans, tomatoes or kohlrabi, because none of them will flourish.

• Fennel will not grow well next to wormwood as it impedes its germination.

Hyssop

Name

Hyssop's name has evolved from the Hebrew *esob* or *ezov*, as it was called in the Bible. To the ancient Greeks it was *hussopus*, a short step from the modern *hyssop*. *Officinalis* denotes its use in medical herbal practice.

History

In *Exodus*, the Lord instructed Moses in the rite of the Passover: when Moses called for the Elders of Israel he told them that each family must kill a lamb, 'And ye shall take a bunch of hyssop, and dip it in the blood that is in the bason, and strike the lintel and the two side posts with the blood that is in the bason; and none of you shall go out at the door of his house until the morning.' This was a sign to the Angel of Death to pass over that house. In later years the Temple was purged with hyssop, and in the New Testament, St John describes how, at the time of the crucifixion, 'there was a vessel full of vinegar: and they filled a spunge with vinegar, and put it upon hyssop, and put it to his mouth.'

For all that, the hyssop of the Bible, *esov*, was a wall-growing plant used in the ritual cleansing of lepers. It was a species of caper or savory, not the *H. officinalis* that we know today. And yet the confusion lingered long, and hyssop was used symbolically in the consecration of Westminster Abbey by Edward the Confessor in 1065.

It was first brought to Britain by the Romans, and was subsequently

Hyssopus officinalis
Labiatae

grown in monastic infirmary gardens: it has naturalized on the thirteenth-century walls of the Cistercian Abbey of Beaulieu in Hampshire. Medieval cooks used it in omelettes, pottages and pickles, and added it to an eyewash made with rosewater.

With its linear leaves and enchanting violet-blue flowers it was used as a hedging plant in Elizabethan gardens. Modern cultivated varieties produce lovely flowers of pink, red or white.

Folklore

- A powerful anti-witchcraft herb, hyssop possesses special defences against the powers of darkness.

- To dream of hyssop means that friends will be instrumental to your peace and happiness.

Folk medicine

Hippocrates recommended hyssop as a chest-herb, and used it in remedies for pleurisy and bronchitis. Over the centuries hot hyssop tea has been prescribed for throat infections, colds and catarrh. It is a powerfully antiseptic herb and was found to combat these conditions quite effectively.

It was also used as a wound-herb: a compress of hyssop was applied to bruises, black eyes and to ease muscular pain. Parkinson described how it 'used of many people in the country to be laid into cuts and fresh wounds, being bruised and applyed either alone, or with a little sugar'. Edmund Spenser described it as 'Sharp hishop, good for greene woundes remedies'.

Cooking with hyssop and other uses

Hyssop has a slightly minty, but a strong, bitter taste, and is not the best of culinary herbs, although it is acceptable used sparingly in salads, stews and

soups. Being a good digestive, its tangy flavour and pungent aroma go well with rich foods such as pork, duck, eel and pâtés. It is used to flavour spirits and liqueurs such as absinthe and Chartreuse.

Both butterflies and bees are attracted to hyssop, which contributes to a superb honey. The herb, being insect-repellent, made a good strewing herb, and it was also used to preserve meat. It has deodorant properties and was used as a cleansing herb. The dried flowers make a delicious tea, the dried leaves can be part of a *pot-pourri*, and hyssop is used in perfumery as a component of Eau de Cologne. It is also a cosmetic herb: 'A Water to cause an Excellent Colour and Complexion – Drink six spoonsful of the juice of Hyssop in warm Ale in a morning fasting', directs *The Receipt book of John Nott*, cook to the Duke of Bolton (c.1723).

Growing hyssop

Hyssop is a native of central and southern Europe, and in the wild it grows in rocky regions, preferring chalk. In cultivation it is fairly hardy and will tolerate most soils so long as it is in a sunny position. It can be propagated from seed, from cuttings or by root division. The seed should be planted in April, and the young plants thinned out once they are well-established, leaving a good space in between. Cuttings or root division can be made in autumn or spring.

Hyssop is an aromatic perennial low growing shrub with woody stems, which can grow to nearly 2 feet tall, and needs to be cut back after flowering. Its blue flowers open from July to September.

Companion planting
- Plant hyssop near a grapevine to increase the yield of grapes.

- Radishes do not grow well next to hyssop.

- Hyssop attracts the cabbage-white butterfly away from cabbage.

- Hyssop is insect-repellent, and hyssop tea can be used on plant diseases caused by bacteria.

Lavender

Name

The name lavender comes from the Latin *lavare*, to wash, because the herb has so long been used to scent a bath. The sixteenth-century herbalist William Turner describes its use to wash men's heads 'which had any deceases therein'. *Angustifolia* means narrow-leaved.

History

Lavender must have been an established garden plant by the twelfth century, as the Abbess Hildegarde describes its aromatic odour and many virtues in a chapter entitled 'De Lavendula'. *Llafant* or *lavyndyll* is known to have been grown in thirteenth- and fourteenth-century monastic infirmary and kitchen gardens. By the fourteenth century dried lavender was being used in aromatics, for in 1387 cushions stuffed with *lavande* were made for King Charles VI of France.

Lavender was much used as a hedging plant in Tudor knot gardens, ideally suited for clipped borders in formal designs, with its beautiful and varied mauves. Queen Henrietta Maria (1609–69), the French wife of Charles I, particularly loved the white variety, *L. alba*, and she grew great borders of it at Wimbledon Manor. Her garden there had 'very great and large borders of Rosemary, Rue and White Lavender and great varieties of excellent herbs'.

The Pilgrim Fathers took lavender shrubs with them to the New

Lavandula angustifolia
Labiatae

World, but reported back that 'Lavender is not for this climate.' However, it seems to have survived because in a Boston newspaper of 30 March 1760 lavender is advertised for sale.

    Back in Europe in the seventeenth century lavender was cultivated quite extensively, as reported by John Parkinson in 1629: 'Lavender groweth in Spain abundantly, in many places wilde, and little regarded that many have gone and abiden there to distil the oyl thereof, whereof great quantity now commeth over from thence to us: and also in Languedoc and Provence in France.'

    Lavender was a popular commodity for the seventeenth-century housewife – perfuming the sheets at the same time as preventing moths – and it was strewn on the floors of houses and churches to ward off the plague. It was one of the herbs used to decorate churches on St Barnabas' Day, along with roses and woodruff. It was highly valued for its antiseptic properties in days of disease and unhygienic living, and herb women sold barrows full of lavender on the streets of London, uttering what must have become a familiar cry:

> *Here's your sweet lavender, sixteen sprigs a penny,*
> *Which you'll find, my ladies, will smell as sweet as any.*

Although lavender was first grown on a large scale at Hitchin in 1568, it did not become a commercial enterprise there until 1823. An acre of Hitchin lavender was said to yield from 12–30 pounds of essential oil. By the eighteenth century the English house of Yardley had a flourishing soap and perfumery industry in London, and their lavender water was and still is a highly successful commercial product. London's lavender fields were then at Mitcham, and 'Mitcham Lavender' is famous all over the world, even today. Although it is no longer grown there, it has left a legacy of street names: Lavender Avenue, Grove and Walk. Other parts of London bear witness to this flourishing industry: Lavender Rise, Hill, Street, Lane, Close, Gardens, Grove, Place, Road, Sweep, Terrace, Vale, Walk and Way.

Folklore

● Lavender is dedicated to Hecate, the goddess of witches and sorcerors, and to her two daughters Circe and Medea. In spite of this it was, ambiguously, used to avert the Evil Eye.

● In the 'Language of Flowers' lavender represents 'mistrust'. It was believed that the viper made lavender its habitat, so the plant must be approached with caution.

● Lions and tigers became docile with the scent of lavender.

Folk medicine

L. stoechas was used medicinally until the eighteenth century, and was included in the British Pharmacopoeia of 1746. It is a good antiseptic, and a lotion of lavender was applied to cuts and bruises, wounds and burns. Interestingly, one of the founders of aromatherapy at the turn of the century, Professor Gattefossé, tells of a severe burn on his hand curing within days after it was plunged into a bowl of lavender oil. The oil was rubbed into children's hair to kill lice and their eggs, and huntsmen were known to save the life of a dog bitten by a viper by immediately rubbing the bite with a handful of lavender flowers crushed between their fingers.

Oil of lavender was widely used for its tranquillizing and soothing effect, both in nervous disorders and for upset stomachs. It was an important ingredient of 'smelling salts', given to revive fainting ladies in Victorian times. Lavender tea was a popular remedy for insomnia.

Pickers in the great lavender fields used to put a sprig of lavender under their hats to prevent them getting a headache in the hot sunshine as they harvested the pungent herb, and this trick was apparently known to William Turner in the sixteenth century: 'I judge that the flowers of the lavender quilted in a cap and worne are good for all the diseases of the head that come from a cold cause and that they comfort the braine very well.'

Cooking with lavender and other uses

Lavender's only use in the kitchen is that the very young leaves are delicious in salads, and the young shoots a pleasant addition to stews and casseroles. Principally it is an aromatic and antiseptic herb, used as 'strewings' particularly during times of plague. It has long been made into *pot-pourri* and aromatic sachets, but its most famed use is in perfumery. Lavender water is one of the oldest of English perfumes, and lavender oil added to the bath is a luxury of refreshment and relaxation. Parkinson used it to 'perfume linnen, apparell, gloves and leather and dry up the moisture of a cold braine'. A confusing combination perhaps, but indicative of how herbs were used in diverse ways by seventeenth-century householders.

Growing lavender

Lavender is a native of the Mediterranean, the Canary Islands, Turkey and Asia Minor. It is now distributed throughout southern Europe, and has been successfully introduced elsewhere, including Australia.

There are numerous varieties of lavender, which include a beautiful white one (*L. alba*), the highly scented English lavender (*L. vera*), a less hardy one most commonly grown in the south of France (*L. dentata*), and *L. spica* which produces the widely used but inferior spike lavender oil. Spanish lavender, *L. stoechas*, was the lavender most widely used by the Greeks and Romans in classical times, as an antiseptic and an aromatic. It used to grow abundantly on the islands near Hyères in France, and gave them their name of the Stoechades. *L. stoechas* has gradually been replaced by the hardier *L. angustifolia*.

Lavender is a perennial shrub growing on a woody stem and thrives on poor, well-drained soils. In cultivation it does not produce seed, so it is propagated by spring cuttings or root division. The plants need pruning to encourage healthy growth, and the flowers are best harvested just before they open in the middle of summer. The grey bloom on the leaves is a mass of tiny white hairs which hold moisture in the leaves – so it

is well suited to dry conditions. Among these tiny hairs are embedded shiny oil glands which give lavender its exquisite scent.

Companion planting

● Lavender exerts a good influence on vegetables planted nearby; it makes them healthier and gives them a better flavour.

● In the Mediterranean, where lavender grows next to Scottish broom, both seem to flourish better than when separated from each other.

Marigold

Name

Medieval man dedicated marigolds to the Virgin Mary: 'Mary Golds' they called them, after an old tradition that says she wore one pinned to her robes. Local names include Mary Buds, Mary Gowles, Ruddes and Golds, and also Summer's Bride. The French for marigold is *souci*, meaning care, because it is such a beneficial herb. Not only that, the word *souci* derives from *solsquier*, to follow the sun, as the marigold's flowers open as the sun rises.

Marigold's generic name *Calendula* is Latin for 'throughout the months'. This is because of its long flowering period and also because the Romans found that it was usually in flower on the first day, the Calends, of each month. *Officinalis* denotes its use in established medical practice.

History

Marigolds have been used in medicine since the time of the ancient Greeks, and they are very likely their 'chrysanthemum', or 'golden flower', which is not the chrysanthemum we know today. They were also well-known in Arab and Indian cultures, and were a sacred flower in Northern India where the Hindus used them to decorate the shrines of their gods. They are still used today in Indian religious and festive rituals.

In the reign of Henry VIII the marigold was called 'souvenir', and ladies wore wreaths of marigolds intermingled with heartsease. This

Calendula officinalis
Compositae

combination had the symbolic meaning of 'happiness stored in recollection'. By the time of the Victorian 'Language of Flowers' marigolds had come to represent grief, because they were thought to have sprung from the life-blood of Mexicans who fell to the Spanish.

The marigold seems throughout its history to have been closely associated with the sun, an obvious parallel in imagery, and Shakespeare in *A Winter's Tale*, describes the morning dew on them as they follow the sun:

> *The marigold that goes to bed with the sun,*
> *And with him rises weeping.*

At this time the marigold was associated with Mary, the Tudor queen whose fortunes were as cyclical as the sun.

Folklore

- The Arabs used to feed marigolds to their finest horses in the belief that it increased the strength of their blood vessels.

- Marigolds are a natural barometer: Linnaeus stated that if marigolds stay open all morning, the weather will continue dry. If they stay closed in the early part of the day, rain is to be expected.

- The marigold is an emblem of a fawning courtier, who can smile only when everything is bright.

- Along with roses, marigolds are a symbol of the bitter sweets that are part of the path of love.

Folk medicine

Marigold is a valuable healing plant, and has been used internally to bring down inflamed lymph glands, and to treat duodenal ulcers. Its external use

is principally in a skin lotion as it heals damaged tissues, so compresses of marigold were applied in country medicine to wounds, chilblains, bruises, burns, ulcers, boils and acne. Another important use was as an eye lotion.

Marigold is also a soothing herb, administered for anxiety and insomnia, and has properties which were found to relieve asthma and bad coughs.

Cooking with marigolds and other uses

The marigold is one of the most useful of all herbs, having a role to play in medicine, cookery and beauty care. The flowerheads when boiled in water produce a yellow dye which makes an effective hair rinse to highlight blond hair, although a puritan streak in the sixteenth-century herbalist William Turner rebuked this practice: 'Some use it to make their heyre yellow with the floure of this herbe, not beyne content with the natural colour, which God hath given them.' Marigold is also used in skin preparations.

Marigold petals make a good substitute for saffron in cookery, and can be added to salads and omelettes, or used to colour and flavour cheese. They are delicious in rice, egg and cheese dishes as they impart a tangy, spicy flavour. They can be used in sweet dishes too, and are an original addition to sweet custards and sponge cakes.

Growing marigolds

Marigolds are natives of the Mediterranean, although it is thought that they could possibly have originated in India. They are now distributed throughout the world as a garden plant, found in the wild mostly as an escape.

They are robust, self-seeding annuals which tolerate any soils so long as they get plenty of sun. To start them off in your garden, sow seed thinly in the spring – and then be prepared to find marigolds all over the place from then on. They are enchanting in the herb garden, their large golden flowers a cheering sight for most of the year.

Marjoram

Origanum spp.
Labiatae

Name

Marjoram is named after Amaracus, a Greek youth in the service of
Cinyres, King of Cyprus. He accidentally broke a vase of perfume and was
so terrified that he fell unconscious to the ground. The gods, however,
took pity on him and in their mercy changed him into the herb that bears
his name – first *amarakos*, then *marjorana*, and then, via the French
marjolaine, marjoram. In Somerset marjoram's local name is Joy of the
Mountain.

Sweet marjoram (*Origanum marjorana*) is closely related to
oregano, or wild marjoram (*Origanum vulgare*).

History

Marjoram was an important herb in the time of the Tudors who made it
popular in England by planting it in their knot gardens. Hill, in *The Art of
Gardening* (1563) describes how mazes were often planted with
'marjoram or such like, or Isope or Time'. It became so much a household
necessity that by the early seventeenth century the pioneers who left
England for the New World took marjoram with them: marjoram tea was
such a part of everyday life that they did not wish to leave it behind them.
During the seventeenth and eighteenth centuries the little pot marjoram
(*O. onites*) enjoyed highly fashionable status, and John Parkinson called it a
plant 'to please outward senses in nosegays and in windows of houses'. It

was an important strewing herb too at this time, and London streets used to echo with the cry

Come buy my knotted marjoram, ho!

According to a historical chronicle, the famous seventeenth-century German physician and surgeon, Fabricius von Hilden, used marjoram to cure a head cold that was affecting the equally famous soldier and statesman Wallenstein during the Thirty Years' War (1618–48). The latter was so pleased that he gave von Hilden 200 gold crowns and had him escorted back to Rostock in his own carriage drawn by four white horses. The chronicle unfortunately fails to provide the prescription for the remedy!

Folklore

- In ancient Egypt marjoram was dedicated to Osiris, the sun god.
- The Greeks believed that Aphrodite created marjoram. She took it from the waters of the vast ocean to the top of the highest mountains where it grows close to the rays of the sun.
- To the Greeks it was the herb symbolic of peace and happiness. They also planted it on graves to ensure the contentment of the departed.
- To find marjoram growing on a grave meant that the departed was happy, and so it was a comfort to the bereaved.
- Aristotle reports that tortoises which have swallowed a snake will immediately eat marjoram so as not to die. On one occasion the sly serpent reputedly removed the marjoram and deprived the tortoise of his defence.
- Culpeper wrote that between *O. vulgare* 'and adders there is a deadly antipathy'.
- Sprigs of marjoram and wild thyme laid by milk in the dairy prevented its being curdled by thunder.

● Albertus Magnus describes a charm *'pour enricher par la pêche des poissons'*: 'Mix Nettles, Cinquefoil, and the juice of Houseleek, with the corn boiled in water of Thyme and marjoram and if this composition is put into a net, the net will soon be filled with fish.'

Folk medicine

Marjoram is generally speaking a good tonic and a settling herb – it soothes the stomach and revives sluggish organs. One source tells us that to smell wild marjoram frequently is enough to keep a person in good health! Gerard says that 'it is very good against the warmbling of the stomach, and stayeth the desire to vomit, especially at sea'. Certainly an infusion of the flowers was a folk recipe to prevent sea-sickness.

An infusion of marjoram is good for sore throats, a blocked-up nose and a cough. Sweetened with honey, it is a soothing tisane to calm irritability and to get rid of a nervous headache. It is said that inhaling vapours from the juice will even help a migraine.

Marjoram oil was believed to be good for rheumatism, as known to a medieval herbalist: 'The oil is very warm and comforting to the joints that are stiff and the sinews that are hard, for it modifies and supples them.' Country people made a poultice of powdered marjoram with honey to apply to sprains and bruises, and old wives recommended marjoram oil to cure a hollow toothache. They even put it in the ears to ease the pain of earache and to do away with singing noises. Some believed that marjoram both allays nightmares and checks bed-wetting!

Cooking with marjoram and other uses

Sweet marjoram's pungency – rather like that of thyme – lingers long in the cooking process and it can be rubbed into joints of meat before roasting, to flavour them. It is an excellent herb in marinades too, and an important ingredient of an aromatic *bouquet garni*. Add fresh chopped marjoram to stuffings or sausages or, chopped fresh or dried, to

dumplings to serve with lamb. The chopped fresh leaves are delicious tossed in butter and cooked slowly with cubed potatoes in yogurt, or added to flavour braised chicory. Pot marjoram can be used similarly to sweet, but its leaves are not so sweet, indeed are often bitter. Oregano is much more pungent in flavour than either.

Use marjoram butter for chicken sandwiches, or try it on baked potatoes. Fresh or dried, it is a superb herb for pizzas and pasta dishes, and fresh marjoram is a very good chopped with basil and sprinkled over a tomato salad – the Clown in *All's Well That Ends Well* talks of 'the sweet marjoram of the sallet'. It complements the delicacy of a vegetable like cucumber or salsify, and gives a beautiful flavour to olives preserved in oil (add a sprig to the jar and let it marinate during the storage period). Marjoram and apple jelly goes well with hot or cold meats, and marjoram scones, made by adding the dried herb to the dough, are delicious fresh from the oven and served well-buttered.

One of the most aromatic of all herbs, marjoram was the favourite strewing herb of Queen Elizabeth I. It dries very well and is one of the chief herbs traditionally used in sleep pillows, nosegays and sachets.

Marjoram oil is used in perfumery and was often sprinkled over winding sheets because of its mythical association with death. Add the oil to a hot bath for its delicious aroma, and for a tonic and sedative soak.

Marjoram attracts clouds of bees in the summer, and the honey that comes from it has no peer. The young flowers give a purple dye, and the juice from the leaves is very good for cleaning up old furniture.

Growing marjoram

Marjoram is a native of Sicily, South-East Europe and Asia Minor, and has been cultivated and grown horticulturally for many centuries, for both medicinal and culinary purposes. It spread to Northern Europe during the Middle Ages and was introduced to Britain in the sixteenth century, when sweet marjoram was also known as 'knotted' marjoram because of the knot-like shape of the spherical, clustered flowerheads. Pot marjoram is a similar herb, but with a less fine flavour.

Sweet marjoram (*Origanum majorana*) is spicy and aromatic, grown usually as a half-hardy annual. It is a pretty bush growing to between 1–2 feet tall. It flowers from June to September with pink, white or mauve flowers. It likes quite a damp soil, but one that is well-drained and nutrient-rich, and it thrives in a sunny position. Once established marjoram will tolerate most conditions. It is best propagated from its creeping rootstock, or from cuttings, rather than from seed, and Gerard advises to water it in the middle of the day rather than in the morning or evening. Pot marjoram grows to a height of about 12 inches and carries white to mauve flowers in July and August. Oregano can grow to a height of 18 inches, and its rose-purple flowers also appear in July and August.

Mentha spp.
Labiatae

Mint

Name

Mint is well known for its peppermint scent and flavour. Spearmint is so-called after the shape of its leaves, and Pennyroyal, also known as Lung mint, Lily-royal and Pudding Grass, was given the generic name of *Pulegium*. This comes from the latin *pulex*, a flea, because the fresh plant was used to eradicate fleas and insects generally – and smoke from the burning leaves had the same effect. This aromatic mint was thought to be a thyme, a belief that lingers in an alternative French name for thyme, *puliol*.

The many different varieties of mint have enchanting local names. Water Mint is also known as Bishopwood and Bishopwort. Eau de Cologne Mint, the *pot-pourri* mint, is also called Orange Mint, whereas Apple Mint or Bowles Mint is also called Round-leaved Mint and Pea Mint. The variegated type is known as Pineapple Mint. Then there is Black Peppermint, Ginger Mint and Corn Mint, and a prostrate variety, *M. decumbens*, which can be used to plant an aromatic lawn.

History

St Luke referred to the 'tithe mint' which the Pharisees were commanded to pay: 'Woe unto you, Scribes and Pharisees, hypocrites! For ye pay tithe of mint and anise and cummin, and have omitted the weightier matters of the law, judgement, mercy and faith; those ought ye to have done, and not leave the other undone' (*Matthew* 23). The mint of the Bible is probably *M.*

longifolia, which grows extremely well in the Middle East and was one of the bitter herbs eaten with the Paschal lamb.

The Greeks believed that mint's smell was that of strength, and Athenians used to rub their arms with it and put it in their baths to strengthen and refresh the body. But Parkinson claimed that 'Aristotle and others in the ancient times forbade Mints to be used of soldiers in the time of warre, because they thought it did so much to incite venery, that it tooke away, or at least abated, their animosity or courage to fight.' So perhaps it was a potent aphrodisiac: certainly cups of mint tea punctuated the thousand and one nights of *Scheherezade*! Mint tea is still offered to guests as a mark of hospitality in North African countries.

The Romans used to scour their banqueting tables with mint before a feast, and the floor was strewn with it so that guests treading on it were stimulated by the odour. They used to weave garlands of mint – *herba bona* or *sancta* – for brides to wear, called a *corona veneris*. Wayward women in Roman times made mint paste with honey to disguise the scent on their breath after drinking wine, which was forbidden by law and punishable by death: wine was for men and gods only.

The mint that is used as medicine, *M. peperita vulgaris*, is a cross between spearmint and water mint. It was not recognized as a distinct species until 1696 by the Essex naturalist John Ray (1627–1705), who defined it as Black peppermint. Within twenty-five years it was included in the London Pharmacopoeia, and is still retained in many national codexes, including the Hungarian. Since the earliest days of herbal medicine mint has been known as a 'kindly, healing plant', and was widely cultivated in monastic infirmary gardens.

Pennyroyal used to be grown in little pots for taking on long sea voyages for its cleansing, antiseptic properties. Sailors used its anti-bacterial action to purify their casks of stale drinking water. Mint was an ingredient of the 'Four Thieves' Vinegar' along with rue, garlic, rosemary, sage and lavender – all potent antiseptic herbs. This was a remedy used during an outbreak of plague in Marseilles in 1722: four convicted thieves maintained that taking this mixture had protected them from infection whilst robbing the dead bodies of the epidemic's victims.

Gerard describes pennyroyal growing by the Thames, where it

'rejoyced by its odour the heart of man'. He also found it growing 'about the holes and pools of the place near London called Mile End'.

Folklore

● In *Metamorphoses*, Ovid tells us that the nymph Minte was beloved of Pluto, and that Persephone, discovering her husband's infidelity, transformed his mistress into the herb that is called by her name: the plant thereafter sought underground waters and partially shaded places, looking for her lost lover.

● Mint is a symbol of virtue because of its cleansing properties.

● Mint is an aphrodisiac, and the Arabs drink mint tea for virility.

● Virgil said that wounded deer sought out mint to heal themselves when they have been hunted.

Folk medicine

Mint tea used to be prescribed in country medicine for a cold, and a decoction of mint was recommended as a wash for sore mouths. The tea was found also to be good for nervous headaches and agitation, and it was believed to recharge energy and act as a tonic. Because it is quite powerfully antiseptic it was used to treat cuts and skin rashes.

Culpeper names up to forty cures that mint can effect, and Gerard's advice verges on the wild: 'It is poured into the eares with honied water. It is taken inwardly against scolopendres, beare-wormes, sea-scorpions and serpents. It is applied with salt to the bitings of madde dogges. It will suffer milk to cruddle (sic) in the stomach.'

Cooking with mint and other uses

Mint is a wonderful appetizer, as Pliny wrote: 'The smell of mint doth stir

up the Minde and taste to a greedy desire of meat.' Mint sauce was a Roman inspiration, and spearmint is probably one of the oldest culinary herbs used in the Mediterranean, mentioned by all the earliest naturalists and herbalists. Its strong flavour is often used for masking less pleasant ones, and is also a digestive: therefore mint jelly is a good foil for young and indigestible meats like lamb. Mint butter is delicious on chops, and mint leaves finely chopped are a finishing touch to a salad. A sprig of mint is traditionally added to a saucepan of green peas or new potatoes while they are boiling, and the peppermint flavour lends itself to desserts: mint sorbet, minted chocolate mousses, and mint parfait to name but a few. Mint is a classic addition to drinks like julep, fruit punches and Pimms.

Mint is an antiseptic herb and a useful insect repellent, used as a strewing herb and scattered on the cottage doorstep to keep ants out of the house. A sachet of mint in a drawer of clothes will keep it insect-free, and they say that a pot of pennyroyal will keep mosquitoes out of the house. In America bundles of mint are packed with grain in store to keep mice and other vermin away.

Peppermint oil is used in cosmetics, perfumes and especially in dental preparations and toothpastes, as it is a breath-sweetener and whitens the teeth. Mint is a common flavouring in confectionery and chewing gums, and is also used to flavour such liqueurs as Crème de Menthe, Chartreuse and Benedictine.

The smell of mint was thought to be refreshing for the head and memory, so Pliny recommended that poets and philosophers should wear a coronet of mint, for 'it exhilarates the mind and is very proper'. So it was a good herb to sharpen the mind, 'a good Posie for Students oft to smell'.

Growing mint

'Plant a little mint, Madam, then step out of the way so you don't get hurt,' as the gardener said to the lady of the house. The best way to grow mint so that it does not take over is to plant it in old sinks or in plastic buckets which you then sink into the earth, or to enclose the roots with roofing tiles or slates – and even then plant it away from other less rampant herbs.

It does not breed true from seed, but spreads from root runners underground. One acceptable way to grow mint is in window boxes or tubs – but keep them very well watered.

Mint is a native of Europe, a perennial herb, but it needs a transplant every three years to regenerate its strength. It likes wet or moist, sandy soils, and a warm, sheltered position in partial shade, growing rampantly in the wild near streams and ditches.

Companion planting

● Chaucer grew mint and fennel together: he had a 'little path of mintes full and fenill greene'.

● The essential oil of mint is greatly increased if it is grown with stinging nettles.

● Mint grown next to chamomile produces less oil, whereas the chamomile will have a greater oil content.

● Eau de Cologne mint enhances the perfume of any plant growing near to it.

● Mint and parsley dislike each other's company.

Parsley

Name

Petroselinum comes from two Greek words – *petros* meaning rock, because it grows well on dry rocky soils, and *selinum* meaning celery, which is a pot herb or vegetable. *Crispum* means curly, describing its crinkly leaf. In the Middle Ages it was called *peterselie* (still its German name) which has gradually modified over the years to become parsley. *P. crispum* is our common garden parsley, but there is also another variety, a single-leafed type, known variously as Greek, Italian, Continental or flat-leafed parsley. Yet another parsley, *P. crispum* var. *tuberosum*, Hamburg or turnip-rooted parsley, is grown for its delicious root. Parsley is a member of the carrot family and a cousin of fennel and celery.

History

The ancient Greeks believed that parsley sprang from the blood of Archemorus, the forerunner of death: according to legend he was carelessly laid by his nurse on a bed of parsley and was eaten by serpents, so to them parsley was associated with death and funerals. They used it in ceremonies dedicated to Persephone, captive wife of Pluto, King of the Underworld. Heart and soul of the earth, she returned to earth from the underworld every spring, so representing both death and regeneration. In later times, Christians dedicated parsley to St Peter when he succeeded Charon as guide to the dead. The Greeks had a tradition of placing

Petroselinum crispum
Umbelliferae

garlands of parsley on their graves, and they even had a saying 'He has need now of nothing but a little parsley', meaning that 'He is dead and just needs a parsley garland around his tomb.'

Curiously enough, parsley was also a symbol of strength to the Greeks. Hercules was said to have chosen parsley for his first garland, and they crowned the victor at the Nemean games with garlands of this herb. Homer relates that chariot horses were fed on parsley leaves, and the Romans believed that parsley gave you not only strength and cunning but agility as well, so they gave it to their gladiators to eat before they went in to fight. They also wore garlands of parsley at feasts to absorb fumes and stop them getting drunk; in this they emulated the Greeks, whose guests at a banquet wore crowns of parsley which were believed to not only stimulate the appetite but also create quiet and calm.

In the Middle Ages in Europe, parsley became very popular and was associated with black magic and superstition: 'Coriander, parsley, hemlock, liquor of black poppy, fennel, sandalwood and henbane burnt together will produce a whole army of demons.' They believed that if you tore up a parsley plant by the roots whilst speaking the name of someone you hated, he would die a sudden death, and today a country belief still persists that if you pick parsley at the same time as speaking another person's name, he or she will die within seven days.

One great historical figure, Charlemagne (c.742–814), approved of parsley. He once ate cheese mixed with parsley seeds on a visit to a bishop's palace, and he liked it so much that ever after that he had two cases of this cheese sent yearly to Aix-la-Chapelle. Parsley was evidently well-known in the Mediterranean: on ancient medals Sardinia is represented as a female figure beside whom is a vase containing a bunch of parsley. This led the great Linnaeus to deduce that the herb originated in Sardinia.

Folklore

● Parsley's long germination is due to the fact that the seed has to go to the Devil and back seven times before the plant will grow. So plant your

parsley on Good Friday to ensure safe germination.

- Never chop parsley when you are in love because your love will die.

- If you dream of chopping parsley you will be crossed in love.

- To dream of eating parsley means that you will have good news.

- In the 'Language of Flowers' parsley stands for 'merry-making'.

- Parsley will only grow successfully where the woman is the boss of the household: 'Missus is Master'.

- Don't transplant parsley because it will bring you bad luck.

- American negroes consider it unlucky to transplant parsley from the old house to the new.

- Some people believe that if you plant parsley in the garden there will be a death in the family within twelve months.

- Babies used to be 'found in the parsley bed' – rather than in the gooseberry bush.

- Wear a sprig of parsley on your stomach, attached with sticky tape or plaster, as a cure for car-sickness.

- You should not give parsley away, it will bring bad luck because you are giving your luck away.

- A glass rinsed in parsley water will break at the slightest touch.

- If parsley is thrown into fishponds 'it will heal the sick fishes therein' (Turner, 1551).

Folk medicine

Both the root and the seed of parsley are to be found featured in European pharmacopoeias, and one of its constituents, apiol, discovered in 1849, was found to be effective in curing malarial disorders and associated maladies. The essential oil of parsley stimulates the appetite and increases the flow of blood to the stomach and uterus, so it has been used as an aid to

digestion and to regulate menstruation. The roots, eaten like parsnips, activate the kidneys and have been used medicinally in kidney complaints and also for inflammation of the prostate.

Cooking with parsley and other uses

In the first century AD Pliny the Elder, who wrote thirty-seven volumes on natural history, said that every sauce and salad in his time contained parsley, so it has been in use for thousands of years. It is a highly nutritious and valuable food with its content of Vitamins A, B, and C, large amounts of iron and calcium, as well as proteins, iodine, magnesium and other minerals. It is undoubtedly the most commonly used herb in European and American cooking – although, all too often, it is used as a garnish and left discarded on the side of the plate. It is worth remembering that it will probably do you more good than the food it is decorating! Parsley can be used in almost any dish, but parsley sauce is lovely with ham, and parsley and garlic butter is the classic way of dressing snails (it's also delicious with mussels and many other fish or vegetables). Chopped parsley can be added to dips, mayonnaises, vinaigrettes, and sprinkled over vegetables; its stalks are a basic of a classic *bouquet garni*. Parsley is a vital ingredient of an *omelette aux fines herbes*. But a warning from Spanish folklore: don't eat too much parsley otherwise you will look older than your years!

Other uses of parsley include making a green dye from the stems – and the best known method of all for destroying the smell of garlic on the breath is to chew a sprig of parsley.

In the Middle Ages parsley was used to make the hair grow: 'Powder your head with powdered parsley seed three nights every year and the hair will never fall off' was the prescription! It is also still said to cure dandruff and clear head lice. It was evidently a beneficial skin application generally, for parsley water was said to clear the complexion and remove freckles.

Parsley has had various other little uses in country medicine – it is a folk cure for rheumatism, and the juice mixed with wine was used as eardrops to cure earache. Parsley was applied to bites and stings, used to cure a stye, and even given to babies with wind!

Growing parsley

Parsley, although a biennial, is best grown as an annual as its leaves and their flavour are best in its first year. It grows to about 12 inches high. In its second year it produces small greenish-yellow flowers from June to August, which must be removed in order to encourage new leaf. It is a native of Northern and Central Europe and was introduced into Southern Europe in the sixteenth century.

Parsley has a reputation of being difficult to grow, because it is slow to germinate, taking anything up to eight weeks. You can try sowing seed under glass in February and planting out the young seedlings in May. Or else plant the seed outdoors from April onwards (on Good Friday if possible – see **Folklore**!). One tip to ensure germination is to pour boiling water along the drills before you sow the seed. Plant it $\frac{1}{8}$ inch deep in partial shade in warm, moist, rich soil which you have worked to a fine tilth. It likes a non-acid soil that is loamy and slightly clayey. Thin carefully as it grows, since the plants require space – they say that one plant should not be allowed to touch an other.

Companion planting

- Parsley aids nearby roses.
- Parsley is especially good for tomatoes.
- Parsley and mint dislike being grown next to each other.
- Honey bees are attracted to parsley blooming in the garden.

Rosemary

Name

Rosemary is *ros maris*, dew of the sea, because it is a native of the Mediterranean coastline, growing on the shore within range of sea spray. Its dewy mist-blue flowers are the colour of the sea, too, although this fanciful notion ignores the fact that rosemary grows quite commonly inland. However the notion is picturesque and adds charm to this beautiful herb. The sea connection is seen more closely in the French and German names, *romarin* and *rosmarin*. An old French name for rosemary is *incensier*, because the herb was so widely used as incense. *Officinalis* denotes rosemary's use in official medicine.

History

Egyptian Pharoahs had a sprig of rosemary put in their tombs to sweeten their journey to the hereafter, and the Romans believed that it brought happiness to the living and peace to the dead. The Romans introduced rosemary into Britain, and it is mentioned in an Anglo-Saxon herbal of the eleventh century that it should be put into clothes chests to keep moths away. Knowledge of it was then lost and it was reintroduced to this country by Queen Philippa of Hainault in the fourteenth century: the Countess of Hainault sent rosemary plants to her daughter Philippa in England after she had become Edward III's queen in 1328, presumably as a rare and useful herb for the royal household. During the Middle Ages a

Rosmarinus officinalis
Labiatae

tradition sprang up of decorating the boar's head at Christmas with 'Baies and Rosemaries', as sung in this carol:

> *Head in Hande bring I*
> *With garlands gay of Rosemarie.*

Country people would present their neighbours with a bunch of rosemary as a New Year's gift, so useful and propitious was this herb, together with an orange stuck with cloves. Rosemary played its part at weddings, too, being a symbol of fidelity and friendship: gilded sprigs of rosemary were stuck into the bridal bouquet, and a rosemary branch, richly gilded and tied with silk ribbons of all colours, was presented to the wedding guests as a symbol of love and loyalty.

The Tudors were particularly fond of rosemary, growing it in their knot gardens for its use in both medicine and cooking. Spenser, poet of *The Fairie Queene*, called it 'cheerful rosemarie', and the man for all seasons, Sir Thomas More, loved it: 'As for Rosemarie, I lett it runne all over my garden walls, not onlie because my bees love it, but because it is the herb sacred to remembrance, and, therefore, to friendship; whence a sprig of it hath a dumb language that maketh it the chosen enblem of our funeral wakes and in our buriall grounds.' Shakespeare, too, associated it with funerals: 'Dry your tears and stick rosemary on this fair corse,' instructs Friar Lawrence in *Romeo and Juliet*. Robert Herrick (1591–1674), wrote:

> *Grow it for two ends, it matters not at all,*
> *Be't for my bridall or my buriall.*

Rosemary is a potent antiseptic and was used as a disinfectant in public places in the days of pestilence and plague. Culpeper describes how rosemary was placed in the courts of justice for this purpose: 'It was accounted singular good to expel the contagion of the pestilence from which poor prisoners too often suffered. It was also especially good to comfort the heart and help a weak memory.' For similar reasons of hygiene, the posy carried by the monarch at the Maundy Thursday

ceremony – when presenting Maundy money to the poor – contained sprigs of rosemary and thyme, both good antiseptic herbs, and was until recently made up by the Royal Herbalist.

Folklore

Rosemary has more folklore attached to it than any other herb, and is practically synonymous with remembrance. 'There's Rosemary, that's for Remembrance', Ophelia's words to Hamlet.

● Rosemary originally sprang up on the steep barren cliffs of Sicily, according to a legend that relates how the Evil Woman of Etna cast jealous spells over the island, destroying love and peace. Mandrake, henbane, and belladonna thrived, fixing their roots so firmly into the ground that only evil could spring from the land. The people of Sicily were in despair, and the sea around the island grew turbulent with anger, but the power of the Woman of Etna was so great that she quelled the ocean's rage. As its last wave crashed on the cliffs a maiden was drawn back into the swirling waters crying 'Remember, remember.' Where her fingers grappled hopelessly with the wet rocks a beautiful plant burst forth, and it was rosemary.

● Greek students used to wear garlands of rosemary on their heads whilst taking exams, believing that the properties of the herb would increase the blood supply to the brain. (Rosemary was thought to expand tissues to which it was applied.) Because it is said to strengthen the memory, rosemary has become a symbol of fidelity, friendship and remembrance.

● Rosemary is a symbol of constancy: it used to be wrapped in white paper and thrown into the coffin at a funeral. In the North of England until early this century, a sprig of rosemary was placed in the folded hands of a corpse, since rosemary is the longest-lasting of the sweet-smelling and evergreen herbs.

● Rosemary flowers are associated with the Virgin Mary. They are believed to have taken their colour from her blue cloak when, during the

flight into Egypt, she threw it over a rosemary bush to dry. Up until then the flowers had been white.

> *The Virgin washed fair linen*
> *On rosemary she dried it.*

● Rosemary grew to the height of Christ, it healed with His compassion, and purified with His grace. 'Dew of the Sea' never exceeds a man's height, never exceeds thirty-three years of age, or if it does it will increase in breadth but not in height.

● Rosemary grows in the gardens of the righteous.

● Where rosemary thrives the mistress is master.

● Rosemary wards off black magic and a sprig is a protection against all evil. It was even used in exorcism.

● Rosemary brings happiness to those families who use it to scent the house on Christmas Day.

● Rosemary brings pleasant surprises to those who grow it.

● In the 'Language of Flowers' rosemary stands for 'Your presence revives me', and an old herbal says 'Make thee a box of the wood of rosemary and smell to it and it shall preserve thy youth.'

● A comb made of rosemary wood will cure baldness.

● A medieval ditty runs:

> *To seethe rosemary in wine*
> *And thou shall be merry and lythe.*

● If a girl put a sprig of rosemary and a silver sixpence under her pillow on All Hallows' Eve, she would see her future husband in a dream.

● Before a newly-wed couple drank at the wedding feast, sprigs of rosemary were dipped into the wine to ensure their continued love and happiness.

● Rosemary was the herb that tried and failed to awaken the Sleeping Beauty.

Folk medicine

Rosemary has been used medicinally since ancient times, the oil featuring in pharmacopoeias, and the leaves featuring widely in folk medicine. The oil, which contains camphor, is good for neuralgia, rheumatism, gout and kidney trouble. Infusions of rosemary are beneficial to the heart and circulation, will combat anaemia and depression, cleanse infected wounds and ease coughs and asthma.

Extravagant, and not to say comic, claims have been made by the herbalists for rosemary. Gerard recommended wearing a garland around the neck as a remedy for 'the stuffing of the head, and cold braine'. Also, 'If thou be feeble boyle the leaves in cleane water and washe thyeself and thou shalt wax shiny.' Rosemary water was a standard remedy for the plague and in *The Wonderful Year, 1603* Decker wrote that the plague had been so bad that 'rosemary, which had wont to be sold for twelve pence an armful, went now at six shillings a handful.'

Culpeper believed that it was good for the eyesight, 'the flowers therof being taken all the while it is flowering, every morning fasting with bread and salt.' John Evelyn rubbed closed eyelids with spirits distilled with rosemary flowers, and it strengthened not only his eyesight but all the rest of his senses, especially hearing. The loss of 'smellynge' was restored by a folk recipe for bread baked on sprigs of rosemary.

Cooking with rosemary and other uses

Rosemary has a very strong flavour and a tough texture, so it is best used as a flavouring, and then the stalk removed before serving. However, the young leaves very finely chopped are delicious with such white fish as halibut, and also with shellfish. The pungent flavour is at its best with barbecue cookery, and it is also much used in stuffings and marinades. Its marriage with lamb is a long and successful one, but it is also excellent with veal and chicken. It is a fine herb for a risotto, and beautiful with baked potatoes. It gives its pungency to aromatic jams and jellies and, finely chopped, makes wonderful herb scones and cookies. It is delicious

with egg and cheese dishes, and is an essential flavour in a *bouquet garni*, as well as being a traditional garnish for a claret cup.

Rosemary is the prince of aromatic herbs and has always been used in perfumery, as well as being burnt as incense by the Greeks and Romans. It was the principal ingredient of a perfume called Hungary Water, an early version of Eau de Cologne. This was made up from a recipe given to Queen Elizabeth of Hungary in 1235, either by a hermit or by an angel – the versions differ – to cure her of dropsy. She fell in love with this potion and used it unsparingly – she was seventy-two at the time and crippled with rheumatism and gout. Rosemary, she claimed, gave her back her youth to such an extent that the King of Poland asked her to marry him.

Rosemary was a strewing herb, a *pot-pourri* herb, and a beauty herb. Rosemary oil in a hair rinse strengthens and darkens the colour of brown hair and stimulates its growth. Rosemary leaves in a hot bath relieve aching joints. The oil of rosemary makes a beautifying skin tonic and is also a good mouthwash for halitosis. Rosemary is an important bee-plant and makes lovely honey – such as Narbonne honey, one of the finest in the world.

Rosemary is antiseptic, so it has its disinfectant uses. It is a good insect repellent, an antiseptic gargle and an effective treatment for bites and stings. It was burnt in sick-rooms and hospitals, and carried in festival processions to avert infection.

Culpeper says that rosemary water was sold by apothecaries as a cure for a hangover. Whether this is effective or not remains open to experiment, but certainly the Chinese drink rosemary tea with a pinch of ginger, as a digestive. It was said that rosemary tea made from the flowers, calmed and 'cleansed the body within . . . and wash thy visage well therein, it shall make thee whole and clear. For it is kindly, for it is holy.'

Growing rosemary

There are many varieties of rosemary, and they can all be grown in the herb garden. There is a rare white one, one with a silver variegated leaf, a creeping one, and types that have widely differing flower colours – a

bright blue, pale blue, pink and a brilliant purplish-blue.

Rosemary requires a well-drained soil and a warm, wind-sheltered position. It likes hot sun, requires very little water and will flourish on the poorest of soils, preferring lime. Although a perennial evergreen herb, it dislikes very cold winters and needs protection from wind and frost, disclosing its Mediterranean origins. It can reach up to 6 feet in height, and has needle-like leaves and woody stems. The pale shoots are covered with soft down in the spring, from which the flowers emerge mist-blue in the wild.

Rosemary seed is slow to germinate, and even then germination is poor so it is best to propagate rosemary from cuttings taken in August, and transplant them in the spring. Rosemary can also be grown as a pot plant. Once established, rosemary needs no pruning other than the culinary cuttings, which are best harvested between 11 am and 4 pm on a sunny day, to catch their maximum flavour. Rosemary had the approval of one of the great gardeners of England, Gertrude Jekyll, who eulogized about it: she loved 'ever-blessed rosemary all over the garden, so that at every few steps the passer-by can run his hand over the blue-flowered branchlets and smell the warm resinous incense on his palm.'

Companion planting

● Rosemary and sage have a stimulating effect on one another.

● Rosemary repels carrot fly.

● According to Pliny the seashore plant alexanders, *Smyrnium olusatrum* 'loveth to live in the same place as rosemary'.

> *The herbe is callit Rosmaryn*
> *Of vertu that is good and fyne*
> *But alle the vertues tel I ne canne*
> *Ne I trowe no erthely man.*

Fourteenth-century manuscript

Ruta graveolens
Rutaceae

Rue

Name

Rue's name comes from the Greek *reuo*, to set free, because of its effective medicinal uses. Rue also means to repent or regret, therefore the herb is associated with sorrow and remorse. It is the herb of repentance because of its bitterness, yet it was also known as Herb of Grace and Herbygrass. *Graveolens* means strong-smelling.

History

Mithradates VI, King of Pontus from 120–63 BC, was a toxicologist who wished to find an antidote to every known poison. Rue featured as an important ingredient of his final, invincible formula. After annexing Roman territory and causing three wars, he was finally defeated by Pompey. He tried vainly to poison himself, but found that he had become immune through his experiments, so he persuaded a slave to stab him. Pliny declared that Mithradates' recipe, for which Pompey sacked his palace to find the formula, consisted only of two dried figs, two nuts, and twenty leaves of rue pounded and mixed with a grain of salt! Rue is mentioned in the New Testament as a tithe, an indication of how highly herbs were rated in those days.

Rue is cherished by the Arabs because it was the only herb to be blessed by Mohammed. He was cured of a fatal illness by the use of rue, given to him by gypsies after his doctors had abandoned all hope of

recovery. Its medicinal uses were appreciated right through the Middle Ages, and it was especially respected for its antiseptic properties and used as a strewing herb.

In July 1760, a rumour in the City of London that the plague had broken out at St Thomas's hospital sent the price of rue rocketing in Covent Garden market: the following day it had risen by forty per cent! The governing body of the hospital published a denial of the outbreak in public journals, but nonetheless the episode is indicative of how townspeople relied on herbs in times of epidemic. Rue was, along with other herbs, strewn in the Law Courts to protect the judiciary from gaol fever, and it was included in the nosegay traditionally carried by judges in court. On the bench were placed bunches of rue as an extra precaution. Little wonder there was a contemporary London street-cry of:

> *Buy Rue, buy Sage, buy Mint,*
> *A farthing a bunch.*

Bunches of rue, Herb of Grace, were used in the Catholic church for sprinkling Holy Water before high Mass on Sundays, as Shakespeare knew: he called it 'sour herb of grace' in *Richard II*, and in *Hamlet* Ophelia offers:

> *Here's rue for you, and here's some for me;*
> *We may call it herb grace o' Sundays.*

Rue leaves, as well as being the model for the Club in playing cards – with its deeply indented, club-shaped leaves – also found its way into heraldry. In 1180 Frederick Barbarossa granted the Duke of Saxony the right to bear a crown of rue on his coat of arms. On October 24 1902 it was announced that the King of Saxony had conferred the Order of the Crown of Rue on the then Prince of Wales. Sprigs of rue are now interlaced in the collar of the Order of the Thistle (thistle and rue = thistle and-rew, patron saint of Scotland). It is included on the coat of arms of Prince Albert through his descent from the kings of Saxony, and of his son Edward, later King Edward VII.

Folklore

● Rue is a powerful protection against witchcraft and magic, and fastened over the door it prevented witches from entering. A little bag containing dried rue leaves, or just a sprig of rue, was believed in the Middle Ages to be a powerful charm against witchcraft. Yet it was ambivalent in its magic powers: it could bless or curse, heal or harm, and could be used by witches in their spells:

> *Then sprinkles she the juice of rue*
> *With nine drops of the morning dew.*

● The flowers of rue are so closely connected with eye treatment that the Romans believed that rue had the power to confer second sight.

● In the 'Language of Flowers' rue stands for 'morals'.

● Rue symbolizes repentance and sorrow: 'He who sows hatred shall gather rue.'

● A powerful liqueur called *Grappa con ruta* (still made today) is said greatly to aid the contemplation of eternity!

● To prevent speaking during sleep: 'Take the seeds or leaves of rue and pound with vinegar till it become a mass, then mix it well in old ale, strain through a clear linen, and let the patient drink it' (physicians of Myddfai; school of Welsh medicine of the thirteenth century).

● Rue grows best if it is stolen from the neighbouring garden.

● Rue is conducive to chastity.

● When gunpowder was first used in Europe, there was a popular belief that if the gunflint were boiled in rue and vervain, the shot would not miss.

● Rue tea was given to children in living memory to cure spots: it worked, but a 'horrid bitter taste' is reported!

● William Turner says that: 'Rue is good to be planted among sage, to prevent the poison which may be in it by the toads frequenting amongst it,

but Rue being amongst it they will not come near it.' Rue does indeed contain toxic substances which in large doses can cause death, but to pin this on the toad is rather unfair!

• Grown near manure heaps or next to a barn, rue will help ban pests from farm buildings, being strongly insecticidal to house and stable flies.

Folk medicine

Rue is an important name in the long history of healing. It was used in ancient Chinese medicine as an antidote to malarial poisoning, and was a traditional treatment for epilepsy. It has been used in folk medicine over the centuries for the relief of menstrual pain, and for disorders of the nervous system. The ancient Greeks believed that rue helped the nervous indigestion of shy people among strangers!

A tisane of rue is an effective remedy for abnormal blood pressure and was used for this during the Second World War. This property was recognized earlier by the writer of the *Lacnunga*, an Anglo-Saxon manuscript herbal, which gives this advice: 'For heart work scatter a handful of rue in oil and add an ounce of aloes; smear with that, that shall tranquillize the pain.'

One of its best-known uses in folk medicine was as an eye lotion. Galen quoted it as a good remedy for eyestrain and headaches, and Pliny said that craftsmen, engravers, painters and woodcarvers used rue regularly as a draught, not only to relieve eyestrain but also to preserve the eyesight. The medieval school of Salerno, the earliest medical school in Europe which flourished in the eleventh and twelfth centuries, taught this epithet:

> *Of use to sight, a noble plant is rue*
> *O blear-eyed man: t'will sharpen sight for you.*

In the sixteenth century the herbalist William Turner knew that 'it quickeneth the sight, stirs up the spirits and sharpeneth the wit'. In

Paradise Lost, the poet John Milton tells how the Archangel Michael made clear Adam's sight. He:

> *. . . purged with Euphrasie and Rue*
> *The visual nerve.*

Between the fifteenth and eighteenth centuries rue was widely used as a protection against infection in times of pestilence. Galen had eaten raw rue leaves with coriander, oil and salt as a guard against infection, and the ninth-century poet, Walahfrid Strabo, author of *Hortulus*, or *The Cultivation of Gardens*, grew rue in his garden at Reichenau for its 'many healing powers . . . to combat sudden toxins and expel from the bowels the invading forces of noxious poison'. Gerard tells how the 'leaves of Rue eaten with the kernels of walnuts or figs stamped together and made into a masse of paste, is good against all evill aires, the pestilens or plague'. Tusser, the author of *Five Hundred Pointes of Good Husbandrie* (1573), wrote:

> *What savour be better, if physicke be true,*
> *For places infected, than wormwood and rue.*

Rue has had some amusing claims made for it by the 'old wives' of the past: that it would cure toadstool poisoning if gathered in the morning but was itself poisonous if picked later in the day. The glimmer of truth in this one is that rue can be poisonous if taken in excessive doses because it contains a toxic substance in the oil, called rutin. They said that it would cure lunacy and insanity, that rue oil rubbed into a lump of sugar would cure hysteria, and that it would heal the 'bitings of mad dogges'.

Cooking with rue and other uses

Rue is hardly a culinary herb, because it is so bitter, although tiny amounts of the young leaves can be added to salads to sharpen them. They can also be used to flavour meat dishes and sauces and, in combination with

juniper, sage and thyme, in the cooking of game. Rue leaves were an ingredient of old mead or 'sack', and are still used as the flavouring of *grappa*.

Rue oil is used in perfumery, and the roots of rue yield a red dye. Rue is a strong insect-repellent, and rue tea will kill fleas. Indeed bunches of dried rue hung in the dog kennel will go a long way towards de-flea-ing the dog.

Growing rue

Rue is a native of Eurasia and the Canary Islands, and was probably brought to Britain by the Romans. It is a member of the *rutaceae* family which numbers more than 900 species, including the orange and lemon trees.

It likes limestone soil which is well-drained, and a dry, rocky, sheltered position in the full sun. It is an aromatic semi-evergreen shrub with a mousey, stale smell and a bitter taste. A hardy perennial, it has yellow flowers which last through the summer into autumn.

Propagate rue from seed, or by spring cuttings, or by careful root division. Prune the shrub back in April to improve its shape – it grows on a woody stem up to 3 feet tall, with a most attractive leaf which is bluey-green, and deeply-indented with rounded ends. It is well worth growing for its colour alone in a herbaceous border.

Companion planting

- Rue does not like growing next to mint.

- Rue and basil do not like each other (see page 39).

- 'Rue and the fig tree are in a great league and amitie together' (Pliny).

Sage

Name

Sage's generic name *Salvia* comes from the Latin *salvere*, to be in good health, after sage's medicinal properties. In the Middle Ages it was called *sawge* which became the modern sage. *Officinalis*, as usual, denotes its official use in medicine.

History

The ancient Greeks revered sage, believing that it would slow down the diminution of the senses, declining faculties and failing memory. To this day – and probably for this same purpose – Greeks serve sage tea in their cafés. Their ancestors dedicated sage to Zeus, king of the gods of Olympus, and it is numbered among the 400 simples of Hippocrates.

The Romans called sage *herba sacra* and they too dedicated it to their chief god, Jupiter, using it in much the same way as the Greeks, believing also that it aided conception. They gathered it with special ceremonial, without using iron tools (it is now known that iron salts are incompatible with sage), 'wearing a white tunic, the feet bare and well washed, having first offered sacrifices of bread and wine'. The Romans brought sage to Britain, and where it now grows freely on verges and roadsides are thought to be the routes taken by the legions. Sage was first recorded here as a garden plant in 1213.

The Chinese drank sage tea, too, preferring it to their own China

Salvia officinalis
Labiatae

tea, and at one time they carried on a barter trade with the Dutch, exchanging sage tea for three times the weight of their own product!

Folklore

● 'Sage the Saviour' was truly believed to prolong life, so healthy a herb was it: ''Tis a plant, indeed, with so many and wonderful properties as that the assiduous use of it is said to render men immortal', says John Evelyn. A Roman proverb says, 'Why should a man die who grows sage in his garden?', and an old English country saying is:

> He that would live for aye
> Must eat sage in May.

● A thriving sage bush indicates a thriving family fortune, and it flourishes or withers according to the prosperity of the master of the house. Yet where sage does prosper in the garden there was a rumour that the woman ruled the roost. Nervous men were known in the past to cut down flourishing sage bushes in case they were mocked by their neighbours!

> If the sage tree thrives and grows
> The master's not master and he knows!

● Sage plants were so highly valued that they need protection from the Devil's familiar, the toad. So it became customary to plant rue, the herb that seems to attract toads, near to sage in order to attract them away from this precious plant.

● Sage is a symbol of domestic virtue, and in the 'Language of Flowers' it stood for 'esteem', because of its medicinal value.

● Red sage never does well unless the cuttings are planted by someone with a 'lucky hand'.

Folk medicine

Sage 'has so many virtues that it is considered by many as a universal healer of all ills', according to an early herbal. Sage leaves with honey were

given to consumptives, and smoking sage cigarettes was said to relieve asthma. The herb was used to reduce sweating in cases of fever, was prescribed for liver diseases, and to ease respiratory tract infections. An infusion of sage was taken as a tonic, a blood-purifier and as a stimulant.

Sage was a favourite Anglo-Saxon simple for a dangerous wound. It proved its antiseptic qualities in times of plague when sage juice with vinegar was a popular remedy. Medieval physicians prescribed it 'fresh and green to clear the body of venom and pestilence'.

The Greek notion that sage was a good herb for the brain lingered on into the eighteenth century. Culpeper wrote that it 'helps the memory, warming and quickening the senses', and sage tea was still drunk in those days to sharpen the mind and improve the memory.

Cooking with sage and other uses

Sage is a good companion to pork, being a digestive, so it goes well with rich meats. Sage and onion stuffing is legendary, and goes not only with pork but is also delicious with poultry, tomatoes and a wide variety of vegetables. Sage, which contains Vitamins A and C, is as good in salad as it is in a stew, and sage butter on boiled onions makes a lovely side dish. Put sage leaves on to a kebab, or make fritters with them. A leek tart can be made with sage, and a cheese omelette with sage is a meal in itself. Try it with Welsh rarebit, or in cream-cheese sandwiches. Various English cheeses are made with sage, as in Gloucester and Derby, and eels are traditionally stewed with sage. Liver *alla salvia* is a classic of Italian cookery, as is *saltimbocca alla salvia*, veal with sage.

Sage dries very well although, being fleshy, the leaves need very thorough drying to become brittle enough to store.

Sage is also a beauty herb, good for the hair, the skin and the teeth. It makes a good hair conditioner which darkens greying hair, and sage water cleanses and refines the skin. It is added to some brands of toothpaste, and in the old days country folk would rub their teeth with sage leaves to whiten them, and use sage tea as a mouthwash. As well as being a beauty herb, its essential oil was used in perfumery, and it was a

herb for health also: sage ale and sage tea are both healthy, slightly sedative drinks which have a lovely aroma.

A sage plant kept indoors will keep a room clear of flies, such are its insect-repellent qualities, yet bees will flock to sage in flower in the summer, and make fine honey from its pollen. These handsome purple flowers give a violet dye which in the old days was used to colour desserts.

Growing sage

Sage is a native of Southern Europe and grows especially well in Yugoslavia where it is collected commercially from the wild. A member of the mint family, there are numerous varieties of sage, some medicinal, some culinary and one highly hallucinogenic. Some are red-leaved, some variegated, and there is a narrow-leaved version and a pineapple-scented sage.

Sage likes a well-drained rich chalky soil, and is happiest in a sunny position. It grows between 12–18 inches tall, and has pale grey-green leaves which are soft, oblong and slightly fleshy. Gerard describes them as 'long, wrinkled, rough and whitish, like in roughness to woollen cloth threadbare'. It has violet-blue flowers from early summer to early autumn.

Cultivate sage from cuttings taken from leggy plants in the spring, keep them indoors and plant them out in the autumn. Eventually the stem goes woody at the base, and the whole plant needs replacing every four to seven years. The oil content of the leaves is at its best in May, so that is the ideal time to harvest sage.

Companion planting

- Rosemary and sage benefit from each other's company.

- Sage repels the cabbage butterfly and improves the flavour and digestibility of cabbages when grown amongst them.

- *Plant your sage and rue together,*
  The sage will grow in any weather.

Tansy

Name

Tanecetum, tansy's generic name, comes from the Greek *athanatos*, immortal, because either eating the herb or drinking an infusion of it were thought to confer immortality. It was therefore also used as an embalming herb, because it retains its strong scent for years and is highly disinfectant. Recently a grave was opened at Harvard where sprigs of tansy had been placed in the coffin, and the herb still retained its aroma after 200 years! The long-lived flowers also sustain the immortality myth: in 1656 the herbalist William Coles wrote: 'It is immortal because the yellow flowers gathered in due time, will continue very lively a long while.'

Tansy has entrancing local names that befit its charm – Bachelor's Buttons, Yellow Buttons, Bitter Buttons, Parsley Fern, Scented Fern, Stinking Willie and Traveller's Rest.

History

Tansy is mainly recorded historically in association with Easter. Tansy pudding was traditionally eaten on Easter Sunday, the idea being 'to drive away the wyndes yt they have gotten all the lent before eating of fish, peas, beanes and diverse kindes of wynde making herbes'. In other words to deliver the people from flatulence. Tansy eaten with fried eggs at Eastertide was meant to purge the phlegm engendered of fish in the Lenten season, and Culpeper concurred that 'the herb fried with eggs, helps to

Tanecetum vulgare
Asteraceae

digest and carry downwards those bad humours that trouble the stomach'.

During Lent in the Middle Ages tansy pancakes were eaten as a reminder of Christ's sufferings, as a bitter herb, and tansy cakes were traditional fare at Trinity College, Cambridge, on Easter Monday and Tuesday until early this century. Pepys recorded that he ate a tansy in 1666, and that it was once tried for High Table at his college, Magdalene in Cambridge. 'The Master of the College kindly answered my inquiry with the verdict that it was too nasty to be repeated.'

Folklore

● In some parts of Italy people would present a stalk of tansy to someone as an insult. In the 'Language of Flowers', tansy means 'I declare war against you.'

Folk medicine

Tansy's disinfectant properties are so remarkable that it was believed that just putting a sprig of tansy in your shoes would protect you from the plague. Tansy tea was a cure for worms, and also made a good gargle to kill bacteria in cases of the common cold.

A poultice of tansy, claimed herbalists, would cure gout and rheumatism, and a decoction was prescribed for internal use in kidney complaints, intestinal spasms and even hysteria. It was used by the old wives of yore as a fertility drug: 'Let those Women that desire Children love this Herb, 'tis their best Companion, their husband excepted' – Culpeper at work.

Cooking with tansy and other uses

Tansy is a bitter herb, spicy and pungent, but notwithstanding this, tansy makes a delicious culinary herb picked young and used sparingly. Finely

chopped and sprinkled over fried eggs its sharpness detracts from their richness, and it is also lovely in a herb omelette. It makes a tangy difference to a Welsh rarebit, and always enhances cheese and fish dishes. Tansy is good in egg custards, makes delicious scones and cakes, and the traditional tansy pudding, a kind of herby crème caramel, is a beautiful dessert.

Tansy is a powerful insect repellent, and used to be rubbed into meat to keep bluebottles away. Hang a bunch in your larder to deter flies, and rub tansy into the dog's coat to get rid of fleas. Highlanders used tansy to repel mice in the farmhouse, and it was used in times of plague as a disinfectant strewing herb, as well as being one of the chief anti-moth herbs laid among clothes.

Traditionally used as an embalming herb, tansy also finds a place in *pot-pourri* mixtures because of its spiciness, and it was used in cosmetics according to the *Virtuous Boke of Distyllacioun* of 1527.

Growing tansy

Tansy is native to the North temperate zones, growing almost anywhere. In Britain it is found on waste places, hedge-banks and roadsides, spreading rapidly with its running roots. Tansy grows about 2 feet tall, a distinctive herb with its bright green feathery leaves and yellow button flowers. John Clare loved 'tansy running high' and tried 'through the pales to reach the tempting flowers'. If you introduce tansy into your garden with a cutting or a root runner, you need do no more than control its spread – it is a plant that happily looks after itself. The hardiest of perennials is unconcerned with the conditions in its habitat, although it does need a moderate amount of moisture in the soil.

Companion planting

● Plant tansy near peach trees to keep away bugs.

● Tansy repels flies and ants, and is also a moth-repellent.

● Tansy concentrates plenty of potassium and is beneficial as a decomposing agent on the compost heap.

Thyme

Name

Thyme's name comes from the Greek *thuos*, meaning incense, because thyme was so fragrant that it made as aromatic an incense as any spice. Its local names include Bank Thyme, House Thyme, Mother Thyme and Shepherd's Thyme.

History

To the ancient Greeks, thyme represented the graceful elegance of the Attic style, because it grew all over the slopes of Mount Hymettus. To 'smell of thyme' was praise bestowed on writers who had mastered the Attic style. The thyme of Mount Hymettus makes legendary honey which has been famous since classical times, and still today has an unrivalled fragrance. The Greeks also used to burn thyme as incense in their temples.

The Romans used thyme too, and although some believe that they brought garden thyme to Britain, there is stronger evidence that it spread north of the Alps between the ninth and thirteenth centuries AD. Roman soldiers used to bathe in water infused with thyme, to give them vigour.

Ladies in the age of chivalry used to embroider scarves for their knights who were about to go on a crusade. A favourite motif was a bee hovering about a spray of thyme, the union of the loveable with the active.

Thymus vulgaris
Labiatae

Folklore

- Thyme is a flower of the fairies and a favourite herb of the elves. Tufts of thyme growing in wild places are the playgrounds of the 'wee folk'. The fairy king's musical hounds will willingly ignore the richest blossoms of the garden in order to hunt for golden dew in the flowers of thyme.

- A Greek legend tells how thyme sprang up from the tears of the beautiful Helen of Troy.

- Thyme is associated with strength and happiness, and in the Middle Ages it was a symbol of courage. In the 'Language of Flowers' it stands for 'activity'.

- It was believed that thyme renewed the spirits of both man and beast.

- On St Agnes' Eve, January 20, place a sprig of thyme in one shoe and a sprig of rosemary in the other, for a vision of the man you will marry.

- Pliny said that when thyme was burnt, it put venomous creatures to flight.

- Thyme is closely associated with death. The souls of the dead are said to dwell in the flowers of thyme, which in England are especially associated with murdered men.

- In Wales graves were often planted with thyme. In Derbyshire thyme was brought into the house after a death and kept there until the funeral was over.

- The Order of Oddfellows carried a sprig of thyme at a funeral to throw in the grave of a dead member.

Folk medicine

The active principle of thyme's essential oil is thymol, first isolated by the German apothecary Neumann in 1725. Thyme has had a multitude of uses throughout history: the Romans used it as a remedy for melancholy, and it was generally believed to be good for lethargy and depression, herbalists

recommending it as a powerful cure for splenetic and melancholic diseases.

Thyme tisane calms the nerves and helps give a good night's sleep, and it is also good for headaches, coughs, catarrh and asthma. It has been used in folk medicine in cases of both whooping and bronchitic coughs. Thyme sweetened with honey is certainly an effective soothing medicine for any cough, and will ease a respiratory tract infection. Generally, it is good for anaemia, and mental and physical exhaustion. Culpeper called it a 'noble strengthener of the lungs, as notable a one as grows'.

Thyme is a powerful antiseptic and was used as a protection against leprosy and the plague. It makes a disinfectant gargle and mouthwash, and a good poultice for wounds, abcesses and burns. Bacilli cannot withstand the action of thyme essence for more than an hour, so it was regarded by herbalists as a cure-all. Thyme ointment is good for spots and pimples, and a decoction is a good scalp tonic. Thyme vinegar is said to cure a headache, and a little branch of thyme in your bath relieves fatigue.

Cooking with thyme and other uses

Thyme is one of the great classic culinary herbs, used to flavour food since man first discovered it. It is an essential herb in a *bouquet garni*, and is the traditional flavouring for jugged hare, as well as being unequalled in an oxtail stew, a *boeuf bourguignonne*, or a *navarin* of mutton. Its strong flavour permeates marinating foods, is superb in wine cookery and gives pork and wild boar a highly aromatic quality. It goes well with these rich foods as it is a good digestive herb, helping to break down fats, and it also improves the appetite.

There is a seventeenth-century recipe for a soup using thyme and beer which, it was claimed, would cure shyness! Lemon thyme is particularly delicious in custards and fruit desserts, and thyme is one of the herbs used to flavour Benedictine.

Thyme is a good moth-repellent, and a sachet of dried thyme is an effective measure in the clothes chest or wardrobe to keep them pest-free. Judges carried posies in medieval times which contained thyme and other

antiseptic herbs, to protect them from the odours and diseases of the common people. An embalming and strewing herb, it has also found its way into *pot-pourri*, herb pillows, perfumes and soaps, and has been used in toothpastes for its disinfectant properties.

The plant yields two dyes, one grey-gold and the other yellow. Thyme is very much a butterfly and bee-plant, and 'thyme for the Time it lasteth, yieldeth most and best honie and therefore, in old Time, as accounted chief'. This is still as true today as it was in Pliny's time, when, translated by Gerard, 'Honey mistresses and such as keep bees hope to have a good yeare, they see the Time to bloom abundantly'.

Growing thyme

Thyme originated in Southern Europe and Asia Minor, but is now cultivated in America and can be found growing as far north as Iceland. It is a relative of balm, sage, rosemary, mint and marjoram, all of which are herbs that bring joy and health. There are many varieties in the family – a rampant creeper, a lemon thyme, golden thyme and many variegated ones with such pretty names as Doone Valley, Lemon Curd, Pink Chintz, Silver Lemon Queen and Silver Posie.

Thyme likes a well-drained, sandy soil or loam. It thrives on sunny slopes in dry rocky places, and is collected commercially from the wild. It is a spreading evergreen perennial with a large number of species – there are over sixty European types of thyme alone. You can grow thyme between paving stones, or plant a fragrant lawn with *T. serpyllum*, creeping thyme. It is easily propagated by root runners or cuttings at almost any time of the year, spring and autumn being the best times. Divide old plants every three to four years as thyme tends to get straggly and begins to lose its aroma.

Companion planting

- Generally, thyme's aromatic qualities are said to enliven flowers and vegetables growing nearby.

- More specifically, thyme repels cabbage root fly.